And She Said No!

And She Said No!

HUMAN RIGHTS, WOMEN'S IDENTITIES AND STRUGGLES

Liberato Bautista and Elizabeth Rifareal
EDITORS

Program Unit on Human Rights
NATIONAL COUNCIL OF CHURCHES IN THE PHILIPPINES
Quezon City, Philippines
1990

ISBN 971-8548-50-5

Printed by Philippine Graphic Arts, Inc.
163 Tandang Sora Street
Caloocan City, Philippines

Artwork Credits

DEBORA SPINI	pp.	vi, 18, 38, 97, 113a, 118, 135
NORMAN BUENA	pp.	xiv, 7, 30, 50, 65, 71, 73a, 85, 90, 107, 126, 143, 151, 162, 178

"... when the heart of the king was merry with wine, he commanded... to bring Queen Vashti... to show the peoples and the princes her beauty; for she was fair to behold. But Queen Vashti refused to come...."

Esther 1:10-12

Preface

"We plan to come out with a monograph on women and human rights. Please write something, anything, about the subject matter."

This was in 1987, when this book started to take shape. Women, representing as wide a range of sectors and involvements as possible, were asked to write something about women and human rights, anything. Contributions, written from different parts of the country, made their way to our desks. Two and a half years later, after a long editorial and production process, this book, *And She Said No!*, is finally available in print.

It was going to be a collection of women's writings about a very general theme, women and human rights. Little did we know, until we were right in the middle of figuring out how to put all these articles together, that we were being engaged in a process of learning about a subject matter which we thought we already had reasonable knowledge of. There was no structure, no specific thrust or objective of the publication, save the general purpose of producing a monograph on women and human rights. Women's perceptions of the whole woman question in relation to human rights are varied, but the essays and testimonies found in this volume structured themselves in a way that suitably projects common themes.

There are no "women's rights" as such. The rights of women must be seen as integral to the corpus of basic and fundamental human rights. They are integral to the human rights of all of humanity. The struggle of women should be the struggle of all of humanity. And the sufferings of women are linked to the sufferings of humanity as a whole. This is the chorus we hear as we listen to the voices of the women in this volume.

The writers of this book trace the story of how women have been conditioned to reject opportunities and responsibilities accorded only to men. They remind us that for centuries, women have been taught to say *No* to conditions that would put them on equal footing with their male counterparts because of the accepted belief that they belong to the less superior half of the human specie. Women have said *No* to education other than home economics, *No* to individuality and identity apart from those images mirrored in the eyes of men, *No* to social responsibilities and decision-making powers outside of the home domain, *No* to deep and fulfilling human relationships other than the conjugal.

The women whose voices are heard in this volume   remind us that women today still say *No*. But this time it is a different and a resounding "*No!*" Women are saying *No* to centuries of domination by a patriarchal culture and social systems which subjugate women to a secondary position, a position of "otherness." Women are saying *No* to a socialization which prepares them from childhood to become "good" mothers, wives, daughters according to models created by the expectations and needs of men. Women are saying *No* to sexist practices that reduce their worth according to the perceived biological inferiority of their sex. Women are saying *No* to a religiosity and theology which fail to remember that men and women are equal in the eyes of God. Women are saying *No* to the notion that the struggle for the liberation of women should wait after the social revolution is won. Women are saying *No* to anything and everything that hinders Woman from realizing her full being as a human person, capable of making choices, capable of understanding that her solidarities are in those forces in society which exist for the emancipation of all and in all forms.

We celebrate the richness of the diversity of experiences and insights in this collection. These essays and testimonies speak of a wide range of situations that women in Philippine society face everyday. Moreover, we are also reminded that even as women are a marginalized sector as such, within that sector are conflicts and contradictions. We realize anew that however different their situations may be, women are bound by one experience, one identity, one struggle. It is in these commonalities and diversities that we are led to a framework with which to place in context the woman question in relation to realities in Philippine society.

Indeed, putting this book together has been a learning experience for us. In the process of editing these materials and putting together a collection of artworks for the book, we have often caught ourselves off-guard and wrestling with our own prejudices and misconceptions, as ourselves being man and woman, or woman and man, among other differences that influence our understanding of the subject matter. For instance, we found ourselves arguing whether to use the plural or singular form of a noun, where each form would speak of a different meaning from the other — "woman" or "women," "identity" or "identities," "marriage" or "marriages." Many were the lengthy discussions on "small details" like what kind of face or body build should the woman in this illustration have to best portray a certain message. We realize later that it is not just a matter of style but a matter of which message we are more inclined to support; that our debates were not just intellectual arguments, but are reflective of inner struggles with our own self-images.

We are not editors by profession. As we worked with the materials in this volume, we tried as much as it was possible to keep the message and style of each article intact. We tried to make use of editorial principles to the best of our knowledge and exposure to such principles. Still we cannot claim that the language and styles used, and the theses supported in each of the articles, would be acceptable and suitable for all. More importantly, we found ourselves working with materials that editing cannot tamper with: life stories of real persons.

Our deepest thanks go to them — these women who have allowed us to take a glimpse of their innermost thoughts, who have made themselves momentarily vulnerable by revealing to us experiences and thoughts and ideas which their predecessors were not allowed to express, nor even think of: Victoria Narciso-Apuan; Rosario Battung, RGS; Victoria Corpuz; Cynthia Dacanay; Miriam Ruth M. Dugay; Sharon Rose Joy Ruiz-Duremdes; Corazon Estojero; Geraldine L. Fiagoy; Nena Gajudo; Carol Gamiao; Emily Garcia; Helen R. Graham, MM; Joy Hofer; Cecilia C. Lagman; Memen L. Lauzon; Adul de Leon; Lorena Lopez; Tita Lubi; Mary Lou B. Marigza; Wilhelmina and Rodolfo Molina; Edna J. Orteza; Marissa Piramide, OSB; Rose Cerdeña-Quebral; Evangeline Ram; Milagros Reloj; Nelia Sancho; Evelyn Balais-Serrano; Carolyn Israel-Sobritchea; Brenda Stoltzfus; Irenea Tayag; Christine Tan, RGS; Adora Faye de Vera; and Erlinda Yandoc.

We acknowledge with gratitude and great honor the forewords written by Sister Mary John Mananzan, OSB and Ms. Mercy Amba Oduyoye. Their grasp of the subject matter, borne out of their wide exposure and deep commitment to the struggles of women, provided a broader perspective in understanding the specificity of the messages in this volume.

This book would have failed to express enough the depth of the theme it is trying to convey without the visual artistry of Debora Spini and Norman Buena, who both took time to read the manuscripts, in their raw form, to draw inspiration for the artworks in this volume. We owe them our special thanks not only for gracing the pages of this book with their artworks, but for sharing with us their thoughts as well. Their contribution in visual art form also reflect their own identification with the collective message of these essays and testimonies.

We also like to thank those who have given us their critiques and reviews included in the book: Nelinda Briones, Robert McAfee Brown, Esther Byu, Anna Dominique Coseteng, Aurora Javate de Dios, Elizabeth Ferris, Priscilla Padolina, June Rodriguez, Debora Spini, and Elizabeth Tapia.

We acknowledge with deep thanks the financial contribution given by friends which augmented the meager local sources available for the publication of this book: the Women's Division — General Board of Global Ministries of the United Methodist Church, the Sub-Unit on Women of the World Council of Churches, and the Women's Concerns Desk of the Christian Conference of Asia.

Thanks are also due to two women, Ruth Lumaban and Doris Rifareal, for providing us with the much needed clerical and technical assistance during the earlier stages of preparing this collection.

Finally, we would like to express our appreciation to Sister Helen Graham for graciously permitting us to use the title of her article in this collection as title for the book itself.

This volume is our humble contribution to the growing library of women's literature and human rights references. It does not attempt to cover all facets of experiences of Filipino women, nor to illumine all the conditions in Philippine society to which women must say *No*. Each of us has our specific *Nos* to say, as one reader of the book puts it, and we hope that this book will be of some help in identifying those *Nos*.

E. Rifareal
L. Bautista

May 8, 1990

Contents

Women and their Place in Church and Society

Women and their Experience of Human Rights Violations

Women and their Struggle for Human Rights

Foreword

SR. MARY JOHN MANANZAN, OSB

These are stories of women about women, of suffering women about suffering women, of brave women about brave women.

They are powerful first-hand accounts of the poignant, tragic, gruesome experience of women of all ages, of malnourished infants, of prostituted little girls, of abandoned street children, of raped adolescents, of raped and tortured young women organizers, of exploited women workers, of harassed miners' wives, of grieving widows and mothers of disappeared husbands and sons, of beheaded peasant women organizers, of gang-raped women political detainees.

The stories likewise tell of courageous Kalinga women who routed exploitative land-grabbers; of fearless wives who indefatigably looked for missing husbands and children; of women awakening to their situation and dignity; empowered women who question the injustices of society and denounce the violations of human rights; of women who defy the threats to their life and to their honor in pursuing the struggle for a better society.

Page after page you will read moving and touching personal testimonies of valiant women. And as you relive their anguish, their fear, their bitterness, their mercy and their horror, you are at the same time inspired and empowered by their strength, their determination, their courage, their indomitable will, their creative persistence, and — yes — even their hope!

As I read through the pages and come to the last testimony I say: I am proud to be a woman — I am proud to be a Filipino woman!

June 19, 1989
Manila, Philippines

Mercy Amba Oduyoye

The human community has entered an era in which women's voices on what it takes to be human are expected to be heard and are heard. Women have extended their involvement in the provision for a qualitative life beyond housekeeping. Today, women critique the quality of life they experience, describe their vision of the new human community, prescribe what could be done harmoniously with the rest of creation, and take it upon themselves to ensure that these dreams become realities. Most women of the Third World realize that, to achieve this new community and new ways of relating to the rest of creation, they must bring to the attention and consciousness of men what it has meant to women to conform to traditional prescriptions for being woman. The human community is now educating itself on these issues. There is now a sign of hope in the mass media where women's voices are heard, their words read, and their presence felt through images other than those of seducers, human beings imaged through their gender and not through what they have to say on what concerns the whole community.

This collection of women's words is evidence that there is yet a lot more to be learnt from women's lives and more to do to bring into being the true humanity that Christianity speaks about. Several themes have emerged as being globally applicable and calling for deliberate steps to be taken universally. Women are human and what they describe as women's rights are human rights. Women say *No* to the centuries-old coping devices that have ensured the persistence of the world's dominant patriarchal culture, with its hierarchies of male-female, animate-inanimate, turning differences into superior and inferior. This contribution by Filipinas concentrates on human rights, giving us real-life stories of women's experiences of its violation by deliberate acts of inhumanity or by simple neglect of what it takes to live a human life. These experiences in their country could be paralleled to much that other Third World women are going through and, to some extent, could be applicable globally.

The challenge is for the whole human community to turn the litany of women's woes into a new bill of rights to guide a new concept of living fully human lives. The personal stories of abductions and tortures debase the humanity of all of us humans. Women have identified the need to see sexism as a political issue calling for action by the whole human community and by each nation. Women who take religion seriously as a factor shaping the ethos of the body politic of which they are a part are challenging the traditional views on women expressed in their faith communities. Control of human beings through the agencies of culture and religion plays a central role in feminist research and writing. This piece is no exception. Violence done to the humanity of the other is violence whether it is done by a member of one's family or by someone encountered in the street. Women have brought together the political, the religious and the familial. They are calling for legal and legislative instruments to safeguard and promote the humanity of all. Work in this sphere is slow, far too slow for the crises in which we find ourselves. In much of the Third World this situation is complicated by the operation of unreformed colonial laws. Women seek to be involved in these reforms to ensure that they reflect the justice for all which they are struggling for.

This volume reminds us constantly of the various levels of meanings of words like oppression, violence, poverty, and power. The writers point to the learnt responses of women to "women's issues" which blind some of them to the outrageous treatments inflicted on women. These conditioned responses stimulate in them a lack of sympathy with those women they have been taught to label "bad." The women writers here make a clear calling for a continued and thorough analysis of all these so-called women's issues, for it is only as we get to the roots that we can understand how the system and structures are fed. We are reminded that each woman has her own personal, interior battle of sexism as it affects her. We are told of stories of how she deals with these issues, how she contributes to its hold on society or struggles for its demise.

Finally, as you read, you will notice how women's issues are community issues and what is perceived as affecting men, affects women and children. This is characteristic of Third World feminism. A graphic example is the exploitation of miners which reverberates on the style of life of spouse and children. The miner's shift regulates the wife's use of her time. One will not be far off the mark to say that this is the experience of many wives the world over: being available has been one mark of mothers and wives while it is not necessarily that of fathers and husbands. There is a lot in the experiences of Filipinas narrated here that correspond to those of women in other countries. With the creation of centers dedicated to research by women on community issues, the global nature of sexism becomes more and more apparent. These centers and the various coalitions for the humanity of women are human development efforts that need to be encouraged worldwide, for the prostituted humanity of all women belies the dignity and worth attributed to human beings. The efforts of women in this direction is therefore part of the struggle to liberate the human spirit to be truly and fully human.

Women all over the world are raising questions that have been on women's hearts for centuries, but stuck in their throats because of their socialization to silence. Now the silence is broken, the feet unbound and the hands put to work for the shalom, not only of the family and the society, but also of women. This is a book on human rights that tells us plainly that "A human rights violation is an act of irreverence, a desecration... that strikes at the center of what being human is all about, for it denies the affirmation that we humans are made in the image of God."

January 26, 1990
Geneva, Switzerland

*Women and
their Place in
Church and Society*

Women: Images and Distortions

EDNA J. ORTEZA

> *Woman, the relative being . . .*
> *the incidental,*
> *the inessential,*
> *Man, the Subject, the Absolute*
> *Woman, the Other.*
>
> Simone de Beauvoir

THE SILENT OTHER

I grew up in silence. My parents taught me to behave, to be decent, to respect authority, to speak only when asked. I learned to be quiet and, eventually, not to speak even when asked. Early in life, I lost the power of speech.

In silence, I learned to hear the rhythm of life around me: voices, footsteps, laughter, the wind, the rain. I wrote poems about leafless trees and empty dreams. I searched the vastness of the sky and implored: Speak to me. You are so quiet Yourself. Are You a Protestant? Are You married? Why do You have a nameless Wife?

As a wife myself, I remained for a long time the wife of my husband and the daughter-in-law of my better known parents-in-law. My world of silence expanded as I bore children one after another amid echoes of repression in the larger world around me. I sought sanctuary in the conjugal sphere, continually getting rid of dirt, rearranging furnitures, piling towels and bedsheets and shirts in impeccable order, aching painfully to put some semblance of order in the growing confusion within me.

As a pastor's wife, I taught Sunday School, played the organ, directed the choir, decorated the altar, designed the bulletin board, served the guests coffee, met with the women, visited the sick, inspired the young. I worked hard and created furiously, but I did not earn. The church council and the congregation appreciated the imagination and the creativity and expressed to me a million times how "perfect" a couple we were. And, I smiled . . . properly, in silence.

Then, there was silence no longer. The rumblings within me became so maddening I no longer cared to fit into the mold of acceptable values and behavior. Suddenly, I wanted to know, to understand, *to be*.

It was too exciting — the precise moment when I discovered the vacuum of my imposed identity; that I was existing merely in the image of the absolute.

IMAGES IN THE MIRRORS OF MEN

Women are stolen souls, mere creatures in a world of repressed fears, longings and desires. Women are pathetic images reflected in the mirrors of men.

> *Chayong*, who farms early in the morning, and washes or irons clothes in the afternoon for more privileged women; who must suffer her husband's drunkenness and occasional promiscuity.

> *Felize*, who, in the comfort of her chauffeured air-conditioned car, talks about her politician-husband

who perhaps spent the previous night with his mistress; and who, raising her penciled eyebrows, says who-cares-if-he-comes-home-tonight-when-I-am-gone-getting-a-noselift?

Mrs. B., who is tied to her homecraft and expensive hobbies, ignoring her husband's infidelity, grateful that, at least, she is well-provided.

Maria, who agonizes for long hours by the phone, waiting but not quite wanting to know what dreaded news it would bring about her missing husband.

Lian, who, three months pregnant with her third child, drags her children on Sunday afternoons to visit their father in detention.

How many women agonize in confused silence? How many remain imprisoned in marriage, bound forever within the conjugal sphere, doomed to torturous housework with its endless repetition: cooking, cleaning, washing, ironing, sweeping, tidying, cleaning, cooking, cleaning . . .?

The more affluent ones find escape from this imprisonment through accumulation of material objects, designer clothes, cosmetic surgeries, travel, leisure, sports. But for the impoverished, there is simply no escape from this immanence, this eternal damnation of being imprisoned in their sex.

ANGER, BURGEONING SEXUALITY AND GUILT

We join the labor force — in hordes, urgently — because while we need to assert our identity, we also need to survive. But our presence in the economic scene is not making constructive changes for us. There is no room for our intelligence and creativity in a society that wants us to be forever young, attractive, docile and uncomplaining. We are still paid so little, our work deadening our senses, boring us to death. While we are participating in active economic production, the burden of housekeeping remains on our shoulders.

So we try something glamorous. We join the movies. But this popular culture only wants little girls with burgeoning sexuality, with passive perfection and the petulance of an adolescent Bardot or Monroe, *mestiza*, projecting an image of feline sexuality. In movies and mass media, we discover that images and distortions take on greater dimensions.

It was too exciting — the precise moment when I discovered the vacuum of my imposed identity

Or we decide to be relevant. We make a commitment and immerse ourselves deeply in a maze of meetings and consultations and community work. We hardly see our husbands in this new meaningful sense of freedom, worth and dignity. We leave our children to struggle with their self-understanding and with their own search for meaning and independence. We come home one day and discover being grandmothers at 39. Who must bear the brunt of accusations, confusion and guilt?

POSTSCRIPT TO SILENCE

It is significant that the turning points in my life are inextricably woven into the patterns of my husband's life.

The year was 1971. It was the height of the nationalist ferment in the country. The strong anti-American sentiment brought together students, peasants, workers, professionals and religious workers in marches and demonstrations. In May, my husband and I joined a demonstration protesting American intervention in Vietnam. Red banners, angry shouting, fervent singing, artists painting murals on Government buildings and city walls pervaded that experience. Approaching the US Embassy, we were stopped by a thick barricade of police and military. I tried to peer through the metal shields, wanting to understand how it was that Filipino soldiers were protecting the American Embassy against us. The national anthem was being sung when suddenly there was a loud explosion. Then, there was the sound of guns and then, chaos. My husband dragged me out of the cloud of tear gas and the maze of bodies around us. Afterwards, as I looked at the wounded, I felt only anger – and shame, for running away.

In 1973, a year after Martial Law was declared, soldiers arrested my husband. They came like thieves in the night, quiet and swift, and took my husband away into the darkness. I was three months pregnant with our third child, still emotionally and economically dependent on my husband. I looked at my children who were sleeping and wondered what I would tell them about their father, in the morning. Suddenly, I felt so alone. Fear and uncertainty gripped me. And at the depth of this fear, I had to think of my husband's safety. At that moment, I knew I must survive.

It took me a long time to wrestle with my anger, shame, fear, uncertainty, confusion, and the longing *to be*. It was 1982 in Mindanao. The reality of oppression and repression around me brought in a new dimension in my life. I met women, youth and men, alive in their commitment to struggle with their anger, fears and longings. I listened to their stories, their feelings, their pains, their hopes and their visions. The innocent questions of my childhood became ultimate questions of justice and freedom, and put my own theology to test. That was when I made the decision to be involved in the lives of these women and men who, amid their suffering, continue to hope because they struggle. They gave me the courage and the power *to be*.

REORDERING PATTERNS AND IMAGES

There are women who are now liberated from imposed identities, speaking about their own oppression, linking up with other oppressed peoples in society. But known concepts and known situations do not adequately represent our own oppression as women, much more our suffering. Something greater, something more profound is needed to encompass an oppression so rooted and so enormous that we wonder whether the centuries of distorted images would be any different for our daughters.

All the current values, all the institutions, all the laws, all the prevailing concepts and ideas about how society should be ordered, how people should live together, what we do with our bodies and our sagging breasts and flat noses — all these are still unshakably male.

We are women. We are not only biologically different; we think differently. We love, think, act and create with a passion and intensity that is purely female. We cannot be imprisoned in our sex.

But while we recognize that all the values, institutions, concepts, laws and ideas that prevail are increasingly becoming inadequate, how do we act? How do we assert our identity faced with all the mirrors around us that reflect distorted images society imprinted on them? How do we open up the possibilities for a reconstruction, a reordering of the patterns and images we see?

We long for order, a state of fusion which will protect us against everything that threatens us. We long for the womb that will protect us, like our wombs that protected our babies when we were carrying them.

We long for a rebirth that is at once liberating and whole. We long for a world that is ready to receive us, a world without mirrors of distorted images, a world that will contain us — our sexuality, our uniqueness, our passion, our fears, our desires — a world we would build together for a free generation of daughters and sons.

...n women...
...t their male

...e sexual inequalities behind
all over the country as brought about by the persistence of
old and the emergence of new situations discriminatory to
the well-being of women. A cursory review of the general
condition of Filipino women based on their contributions
show some very disturbing developments.

Gender Inequality and Its Supporting Ideologies in Philippine Society

CAROLYN ISRAEL-SOBRITCHEA

CONDITIONS OF GENDER INEQUALITY

Results of scientific studies conducted during the past few years increasingly belie the popular belief that sexual equality exists in this country. The researches of the National Commission on the Role of Filipino Women (1980; n.d.), and scholars like Cortez (1975), Illo (1977), Rojas-Aleta., et.al. (1977), Bautista (1977), Miralao (1984), and many others suggest that the majority of Filipino women today are not exactly on equal footing with their male counterparts.

Conditions that perpetuate sexual inequalities abound all over the country as brought about by the persistence of old and the emergence of new structures discriminatory to the well-being of women. A cursory review of the general condition of Filipino women based on the foregoing studies show some very disturbing developments.

Gender Inequality in the Economic Field

Women are still left out in many areas of occupations and do not enjoy comparable employment opportunities, privileges and benefits. Many women workers are left open to displacement and marginalization by large firms and subjected to many regulatory policies by government [Miralao, 1984]. The conditions prevail despite the continuous rise of female participation in the labor force, both in the agricultural and industrial sectors, and in both formal and informal economies. Figures show that total female participation in the labor force was 38 percent in 1984 compared to only 33 percent in 1971 [NEDA, 1985:633; Philippine Almanac: A Handbook of Facts, 1973:247].

Available research data also indicate that wages received by women are generally lower than those received by men. The National Commission on the Role of Filipino Women (NCRFW) notes that while the average weekly earnings of male and female workers increased over the past years, the latter's income is on the average lower than that of male workers. The income disparity is most evident in agriculture where the women's average weekly income is one-third lower than the men. The Commission estimates that in all occupational sectors, the female worker gets only 35 percent of every peso paid to the Filipino worker. Meanwhile, the findings of Rojas-Aleta, Silva and Eleazar [177:xii] show that during the last decade, salaried and self-employed women earned 44 percent and 31 percent less, respectively, than their male counterparts.

While more and more women are entering the labor force, traditional patterns of sexual division of domestic chores remain prevalent. Filipino women still shoulder virtually all domestic chores. They spend eight to twelve hours a day of housework depending on such factors as family size, type of community and their own employment status [Miralao, 1984:61]. An increasing number of them are, therefore, saddled with the dual responsibility of earning a living and managing a home at the same time.

Female housework and participation in the informal economy usually go unrecorded in standard labor force accounts. More often, they simply form part of unpaid family labor [Sobritchea, 1984:65].

Recent developments in the agricultural sector intensify the displacement of female labor. Such developments include the introduction of mechanized farming and direct-seeding techniques of cultivation. Traditional female tasks such as transplanting, harvesting and threshing are being taken over by mechanized operations which force many rural women to seek alternative sources of livelihood outside their communities. Bautista and her associates [1986] observe that in Bulacan, women's participation in rice production are generally confined to weeding, reaping and stacking. In other rural areas the displacement of female labor to agriculture is caused by the excess of "cheap" male labor coming from landless farmers.

Gender Inequality in Law and Politics

The status of Filipino women before the law also shows the absence of sexual parity in Philippine society. Even the 1986 Constitution, which claims to be the most pro-women among all previous charters of the country, still glosses over many actual and potential sources of sexual inequalities. GABRIELA [Sancho, 1987] takes issue with the narrow definition of sexual equality and the vagueness with which the rights of women are spelled out in the Charter. However, the repeal of anti-women laws is probably more crucial to the improvement of women's legal status. These are laws embodied in the civil code which pertain to marriage, legal separation, the right to engage in a profession, to own property, to work, to protect one's health and life, and others.

In the field of politics, women clearly come second to men. The number of women who are occupying leadership positions in all levels of government is minimal [Cortez, 1975; Castillo, 1979; NCRFW, n.d., 1985]. In 1980, only

6.94 percent of all gubernatorial and vice-gubernatorial posts were occupied by women. They also occupied only 6.1 percent and 5.6 percent of the mayoral and vice-mayoral posts, respectively. Of the total number of positions in the *Sangguniang Panlalawigan* (provincial consultative body), six percent were occupied by women, and in the *Sangguniang Bayan* (municipal consultative body), 8.7 percent. At present, the same pattern prevails. Women still constitute the minority in all levels of political offices, including the Houses of Senate and Congress.

Gender Inequality in the Home

Recent data show that sexual inequality also exists in the home, the place traditionally known to be the bastion of female power and dominance. Contrary to popular belief, housewives do not play the most decisive role in decision-making in view of their secondary role in providing for the family's economic needs [Sobritchea, 1987]. Bautista's study [1977] indicates that while it is true that 90 percent of all Filipino housewives hold the purse string, not much power goes with it.

> When asked whether they decide on purchases of items like appliances, furnitures, etc., only 16% of wives make the decision while 39% of decisions are made by husband alone. In 45% of the homes, husband and wife decide jointly. A similar trend is apparent in decisions on business and investment. [Ibid. 2-22]

In many instances, the social well-being of housewives and other female family members is undermined by the persistence of such cultural practices as the "*querida* system," wife-beating and corporal punishment of children. The responsibilities of childcare and managing the home, which weigh more heavily on women's shoulders, often cause physical and emotional stresses leading to various diseases and psychological problems. Malnutrition and psychosomatic illnesses are more prevalent among women than men, regardless of income status and age group.

IDEOLOGIES THAT SUPPORT SEXUAL INEQUALITY

Prevailing cultural beliefs, values and norms function to maintain the low status of women in our society today. Systems of social inequality are partly maintained by ideas that justify the unequal distribution of power, privilege and prestige. These ideas, which usually appear as cultural guidelines for social action and interaction, assume an ideological function or become an ideology when they serve to support, maintain and enhance any form of social hierarchy, be it class, ethnic or gender hierarchy.

Perceived contradictions between family life and public life purports that...

Gender ideology is a specific type of ideational distortion which functions to legitimize and enhance the unequal status of man and woman. In societies where women are totally subordinate to men, patriarchy serves as the dominant ideology. It embodies a complex set of ideas which normally invoke mythical biological justifications for men's political and economic dominance over women and their continuing control over women's lives.

The Ideology of Female Nature

In the Philippines, the legitimization of male dominance in the household, in work, in politics and in other areas of life is rooted in the people's belief that men and women have distinct biological traits which are decisive in defining their roles and status in society. Filipino women are generally perceived as physically weaker, shorter and smaller in body size than men. These biological givens support prevailing cultural traditions that mandate women to do "light work" and engage in "less risky" occupations. Work popularly considered as light and, therefore, feminine largely consists of such domestic chores as childcare, cooking, laundering, ironing, dusting of furnitures, and the like.

The value statement that "women are good only for the home" underscores the common perception that women are biologically cut out and better suited for childcare and housekeeping than men. Because she is believed to be physically weaker, the woman's rightful place should, therefore, be in the home where she supposedly performs light work and is better protected from harm and danger.

While the belief in women as the weaker sex easily justifies the prevailing division of domestic chores, it also legitimizes the discrimination of women in occupations perceived as physically taxing. In many rural communities, fishing, plowing, wood carving, carpentry, building, road construction, and even automobile driving are considered *... family interests and welfare are undermined whenever a married woman engages in non-household activities* heavy work and, therefore, better suited for men. In general, those defined as heavy work have higher pay scale, giving men greater economic advantage over women.

The people's perception of light or feminine and heavy or masculine work does not often tally with facts. Recent studies [Miralao, 1980; Sobritchea, 1987] show that rural women generally spend longer hours of work than men. Their domestic work in the informal economy are equally, if not more, physically taxing since many "male" activities such as farming and fishing are now greatly lightened by labor-saving technologies.

Cultural practices regulating the physical mobility of women also find justification in the belief that women are weak and cannot, therefore, protect themselves from physical harm. Unlike their male counterparts, rural females, especially the young ones, do not roam freely within and outside the village. They are taught to stay at home most of the time and limit their physical activities to places close to home. They are expected to ask permission when going out and are refrained from staying out late at night. By the time girls grow up and these restrictions ease somehow, they are already well socialized into limiting their physical movements within publicly acceptable confines. The end result is that women do not participate as actively as men in public or non-domestic activities, nor in decision-making affairs that affect political and economic life.

The innate qualities perceived to differentiate the sexes are not only limited to biological traits. Filipinos in general also attribute men and women with distinct behavioral and intellectual characteristics.

Whether true or purely illusory, these stereotyped ideas also function to rationalize the prevailing patterns of sexual distribution of power and material resources. Filipino males are generally perceived to be brave, alert, decisive and highly responsible [Santiago, 1982]; while females are stereotyped as emotional, sensitive, indecisive and talkative. Housewives are particularly stereotyped as nagger and temperamental.

Although many of these sexually-linked stereotyped traits are harmless in the sense that they do not have any immediate effect on the status of the sexes and on their access to political and economic opportunities, some influence recruitment preferences and work policies. They set the general conditions for the acceptance of social practices discriminatory to women. For example, the belief that men are more decisive and less emotional than women underlies this society's preference for male economic managers and political leaders.

The Primacy of the Female Reproductive Role

In addition to the ideology of female nature, a host of other beliefs binding women to their traditional roles as housekeeper and childcarer is nurtured in Philippine society. An example is the belief in the primacy of the female reproductive role over her other roles in society.

One of the most important cultural values of Filipinos is the desire for children. This value underlies popular aspirations like good health, long life, happy marriage and material prosperity. Most Filipinos desire a college degree and work hard to provide a better life and brighter future for their children. Because of the high value Philippine society places on having children and raising them properly, many Filipino women spend practically their entire lives preparing to be and performing the role of an ideal wife, mother and housekeeper. To some, this means foregoing higher education and pursuing a professional career, or becoming less active in community activities.

This love for children leads many Filipinos to give so much importance to the female reproductive role. Female socialization puts great emphasis on the formation of values and the development of behavioral traits that make for a good wife, mother and housekeeper. An ideal woman in Philippine society is someone who is willing to forego her personal development and, if necessary, suffer all kinds of hardship for the sake of her children and spouse. She is also someone who is kind, hardworking, loving, neat and always supportive of the plans and aspirations of her husband.

When things do not work out according to these ideals, Filipino women would view this as a failure and take the blame on themselves. Adul de Leon [1987] attributes this to the kind of socio-cultural conditioning which leads women to "self-flagellate," in the same manner that other people would point an accusing finger at them for supposedly causing their own misfortunes in life. De Leon says:

> They (the women) too are victims, because this conditioning makes them appear as criminals as when we hear people remark about a battered wife, "*kasi* nagger *siya* (because she is a nagger)," or a rape victim, "*kasi ang seksi niyang magdamit* (because she wears sexy dresses)," or a prostitute, "*kasi hilig niya iyon* (because she likes doing it)," or "*kasi tamad siya* (because she's lazy)."

15

The Separate Domains of Family and Public Life

Another prevalent belief which functions to maintain the existing sexual division of labor and sexist practices in the country pertains to the perceived contradictions between family life and public life. Basically, this belief purports that family interests and welfare are undermined whenever a married woman engages in non-household activities. When faced by a choice, she is expected to put family concerns above all other concerns and activities.

Most people clearly delineate the spheres of home and public life. Home life basically encompasses all activities that involve the immediate family members regardless of whether such activities are done inside or outside the home. Female public life, on the other hand, includes everything that falls outside the "home domain." It includes participation in neighborhood affairs, attendance in church rituals, gainful employment, and involvement in politics. Although Filipino women can easily move from one world to the other, so to speak, many are conscious of keeping these two domains distinct and apart. In the event that there is a perceived conflict between them, family interest readily takes precedence over the other. In their list of priorities, women put children and husband before work and personal career, politics, and all other social activities.

In general, unorganized women hardly see the value of social involvement in the ultimate improvement of their family life. Many still fail to relate the economic and political development around them with what is happening inside their homes. Unless efforts are exerted to alter these ideas, it would be difficult to achieve sexual parity and to make women more active participants in national development.

CONCLUDING REMARKS

The NCRFW [n.d. 34] sums up the general condition of Filipino women today in the following manner:

She forms part of the labor force, encouraged by a favorable educational picture, yet finds herself discriminated against in hiring procedures and getting less pay for equal work with men. Her individual worth is well recognized but economic consideration as housewife go unrecorded in GNP figures. The "sideline" business for which she is inevitably known, as well as ordinary employment, place a low second in her scale of priorities since home and family are expected to take clear precedence. Her contribution to raising family incomes is clear to any observer, yet development and training programs focus on her husband as the target of farm modernization.

Cultural beliefs and practices that function to legitimize the existing sexual division of work and privileges prevail in our society today. These cultural forms allow people to take sexist ideas and practices as natural and in keeping with the normal order of life. It is important to address the issue of sexist ideology for genuine women's liberation to succeed in this country. It is also necessary to destroy the structures that give life to and nourish sexist ideas. In more concrete terms, this means integrating the woman question with the basic problems of Philippine society. It means linking women's liberation with the struggle against class and state oppression.

Women's Rights Are Human Rights
A Perspective for the Philippine Women's Movement

ADUL DE LEON

The struggle for women's rights by all women the world over is a struggle for human rights. Unfortunately, it is rarely seen as such. This is true in the Third World, especially in repressive societies, and even in liberal democracies in the First World.

In the course of power struggles throughout history, societies create institutions to maintain a political status quo. The state and the church are such institutional creations. They coexist in tension in whatever political context, democratic or not, with human beings caught in-between.

To maintain the status quo, the church and the state both exercise power over a single body of constituents through their respective agencies in the name of social or spiritual control. Unhappily for these constituents, but conveniently for church and state, the lines of social and spiritual control contravene, disguise, or support each other — whichever is publicly acceptable or politically expedient at the moment.

At the bottom of this power play are women. They experience its worse effects.

The forces of spiritual and social control heaped upon women violate their human rights through overt and covert forms of "social control." These forces spiritually coerce and deceive them into abdicating authority and autonomy over their own bodies and lives. They impose on them severe forms of systemic and institutionalized violence in the name of "decency" or "moral, spiritual control." Such forces came in the advent of slavery and private property, and of Judeo-Christianity, Judaism, Buddhism, Islam, capitalism and imperialism.

Violence against women is committed for centuries by government, church and society in the name of morality. In its overt and covert forms, violence can be camouflaged under moral values such as "order" and "decency" and thus defocus the culpability of its perpetrators. Inflicted through government and church sanctions, social pressure and stigmatization, camouflaged violence strips woman of her voice and deadens her sense of outrage.

Violence against women, especially in the Third World, constitutes a long list of crimes against human rights: rape, incest, wife-beating, bride-burning, forced marriages, prostitution, pornography, forced motherhood, compulsory sterilization, genital mutilation and castration, medical brutality, rape as torture of female prisoners, sexual harassment, discrimination against non-virgins, unmarried mothers and lesbians, life-threatening work conditions in women-intensive multinational industries. All these crimes are committed in the name of "control," "decency," capitalist profit.

For Third World women working on issues of against women, the task is fraught with probler from the very start. Resistance to tackle issues of violence against women come from women themselves.

This resistance from women, women activists included, stem perhaps from non-acceptance or disbelief of the term "violence against women." The word "violence" is graphic, strong and fearsome. In the Third World, there is an abdication of personhood and an acceptance of the "externality" of violence: that violence has to come from someone else, that it is *done to* women, that it has to be inflicted, that women's oppression therefore is not intrinsic to one's simply being a woman.

Therein probably lies one of the many reasons of our difficulties in working on issues of prostitution, contraception, abortion, rape-in-marriage, pornography, and many other related women's issues that involve female sexuality.

At a screening of a documentary on prostitution, women in the audience elicited reactions of disgust, aversion and shock. Rare was the sign of sympathy or outrage. Or even pity, from which a more solid basis of unity can be developed in the organization of women. The dominant expressions of disgust and aversion from the women reflect a culturally-imposed division of women from women. The range of reactions from the judgmental "how bad!" or "how dirty!" to the self-righteous "I can never do that!" or the separatist "I am not like that!" to the arrogant "Thank God, I'm different!" only reveal guilt-ridden thoughts.

Sadly, all these manifest a false sense of security and a survival tactic among women. They reinforce the particular phenomenon termed in progressive women's literature as the "madonna-whore syndrome." This exists in any culture where women are dichotomized into "good" or "bad," madonnas or whores, depending on the perception of her sexuality, public behavior, sex life, conformity or non-conformity to social mores, and even her manner of dressing and walking, or the color of her lipstick.

Despite criticisms and fears of being divisive or separatist, the Philippine women's movement finally gained recognition as "integral, distinct and vital" to the national democratic struggle for social change in Philippine society. Winning this recognition was not easy, however. Many a battle and argument are being waged by women within movements for social change against blatant or covert patriarchy, ideology, methods and tactics discriminative of women as regards their role and place in the people's struggle.

Methods and styles of women activists in the Philippine women's movement encounter criticisms from non-feminist activists that it is "too feminist," or from the progressive feminists, that it is "not feminist enough" — the classic dilemma of damned-if-you-do-and-damned-if-you-don't.

A painful and infuriating criticism comes from fellow activists who caricature and typecast prostituted women as "lumpen proletariat," i.e., unreliable, vacillating and subvertible by the Right, and therefore ranked last in organizing priority. To them, work around issues of prostitution and violence against women does not, in the main, "advance the struggle." This criticism perhaps stems from inadequate scientific social investigation, hardline dogmatism and lingering patriarchy within such movements. How can any movement fighting for the rights of the oppressed ignore the plight of the most oppressed?

It is evident that education within and without the Philippine women's movement and within and among forces of national liberation is imperative. Consciousness-raising among women and men must be extensive and intensive. Big and small "speak-outs" must be conducted nationwide for women to get together, to be among women, to open up, and to discuss and reflect on their condition. Two processes are vital to these "speak-outs:" reflection and analysis. Discussions have to be carried out systematically to arrive at an analysis that is systematic and political. Only then can issues, goals, objectives and priorities be identified clearly.

Organizing women starts with the conscientizing and training of women activists. This must be done before any broad grassroots education or middle-class alliance attempt is made. It must also concentrate on research, data and method. Women's situationers must be supported by facts and figures. The national profile of Filipino women must be composed, or updated and amplified. A Third World or Philippine women's ideology must be formulated or promulgated, constantly keeping in mind the cultural differences between the Third World woman identity and Western feminist theory, and the tactical ideological differences between First and Third World women's struggles.

Finally, yet paramount, the Philippine woman-activist must become a feminist. The Philippine women's movement must develop its feminists: feminist cadres who can defend a women's ideology within the liberation movement; feminist frontliners who can discuss Philippine issues in ruling class enclaves and on the streets; feminist personalities who can discourse at par with feminists of other countries.

Locally, in addition to reaching its grassroots women, the Philippine women's movement must refine alliance work among its middle classes. Here is where feminism and women's issues have a decided advantage over other political work. "Women's issues" have an emotional and unifying appeal that can facilitate political work across classes. Foresight and the much-maligned "women's intuition" can suggest strategic "entry points" for women education and mobilization.

The pacing of political work, too, cannot be over-emphasized. Political activists, be they women or men, are overly impatient to ground conscientizing to political ideology. The Philippine women's movement must be given sufficient time to dwell on the "personal" because this is the key to women's unity and action. The involvement of women in great numbers waging campaigns on multifarious issues will then impel and necessitate the definition of the movement's ideological line.

The present Philippine women's movement must prove its worth by emphasizing the unique combination of at least two types of political work: reformist and revolutionary. Reformist strategies are those which are mainly welfare service-oriented, which do not affect existing structures, and whose political philosophy do not challenge or recognize the oppressiveness of existing structures. Revolutionary strategies do not aim to work within the present system; its methods are confrontational, interventionist, pressurizing, and attempt to build alternative structures. Reformist strategies address themselves only to the symptoms and not the systems. But revolutionary strategies require an enormous amount of effort and risk, including a broad mass base.

Lobby work for legislative change; consciousness-raising of media, cultural institutions, political organizations and trade unions; women networking; and advocating women's development programs in government are necessary in the work of the Philippine women's movement. To distinguish which strategies or combination of the two types of political work are most effective in building better alliances is also important.

As in other women's movements around the world, the Philippine women's struggle should embody two long-term goals — equality and empowerment.

Women's struggle for equality must emanate from every woman's realization of her state of oppression and disempowerment: to have the courage to speak out and the humility and sensitivity to find

It is not enough for a woman to claim she is feminist or liberated...

the link to her sisters, and finally, to wage her individual, personal struggle in single steps — dangerous and not easy, but liberating.

It is not enough, hypocritical even, for a woman activist to shelter under the wings of the women's movement, even to claim she is feminist or liberated just because she works in the women's movement, unless she wages her own personal battle in her loves, life and work. To the woman activist, the political must be personal.

The empowerment called for by the women's movement is an equalizing of an imbalance and not a domination over others. It is first, in the personal, the development in women of a sense of internal strength and confidence to face life and the freedom of choice. In the political, it is for women to share authority and the position to direct social and structural change.

Any liberation movement must address the personal. Strict religious and social codes of Third World countries enforce ruling class policies regarding issues that seriously affect women's lives and health, sexual autonomy, earning power, social status and sense of self-worth. Issues that affect relationships and the perception and exercise of women's sexuality must be confronted. These include pre-marital and extra-marital relations, lesbianism, abortion, prostitution, and child support.

Within these aspects of women's lives, women's human rights are continually violated. Policy-makers of political movements must formulate policies that reflect the movements' stand on these issues. Programs that provide solutions to personal problems must be evolved. Both their causes and solutions are after all basically political. Policies are especially necessary in a women's liberation movement where the lack of an ideological policy affect women's lives directly. The Philippine Left must realize this and address

... unless she wages her own personal battles in her loves, life and work

women's issues with its wealth of experience and theory. It is imperative for the Philippine Left to undertake this task if it is to harness the full potential of women force. Only then can it earn the distinction of becoming a truly representative political movement. A movement that does not address the personal falls short of being a political movement.

The Philippine women's movement has the unique advantage of being waged within a people's liberation movement.

Its struggle for gender equality can link with the Filipinos' struggle against imperialism. It can initiate tactical single-issue methods on concerns like mother's health, breastfeeding, prostitution, AIDS, women trafficking, and other issues which can be rooted in and raised to the level of ideology.

This approach can lend the Philippine women's movement its uniqueness and creativity, or what the Philippine Left calls its "distinct" character.

The ideology of feminism can contribute creative ideas, new forms and insights, and add greater dimension to a people's struggle. For example, the Philippine women's movement, whose struggle is waged simultaneously within and without the national liberation movement, is distinctly advantaged to challenge and attack patriarchy and the reactionary tendencies of the church at an earlier stage than the national liberation movement can. It must do that now and not be held back by any strategic historical agenda.

The women's struggle, therefore, is not only "vital" and "integral" but crucial to any national liberation struggle.

Both women and men within the national liberation struggle must take up issues of violence against women because these are unifying, concrete and demonstrable.

Men, revolutionaries or not, who do not take action against the oppression of women, themselves support and encourage systems oppressive to women. Women are coming to realize that sisterhood is the shining bond that finally will help break the chains of imperialism, capitalism, racism and patriarchy.

—

Women in Philippine Society

NENA GAJUDO

The assumption to office of a (first) woman-President of
the Republic should be a much needed respite for women
and for a people who suffered much under a dictatorial
regime. It should be a score for women who are struggling
to be counted as humans with all their inherent rights.
After all, it takes a woman to really understand the woman
question.

True, she was the wife who suffered from state
persecution inflicted on the husband; the woman who
animated the husband's battlecry; the woman persuaded
to run for presidency due to a million signature petition,
and succeeded due a citizenry overwhelming with anti-
dictator sentiments. But the woman-President, it seems,
was reared far from the milieu of the women's movement.

True, the 1987 Constitution of the Republic guarantees
equal rights to women. But written law is not necessarily
the same with practice. At once it is ambiguous as to who

interprets the law and to whose interests laws are made. Take for instance the nuclear-free provision in the new Constitution. By encouraging members of Congress to take her "open options" policy on the US military bases, the woman-President is in effect going against this Constitutional provision. Indeed, having a woman-President in an almost all-male cabinet, notwithstanding the machinations of imperialist powers, is no guarantee for women to hold up half of the sky.

"Baby, you have a long way to go" is the subtle message to women. Indeed, to be concerned with issues of human rights and to belong to that specie called woman can be doubly taxing — physically and spiritually.

It is consoling to know that before the coming of the Spanish *conquistadores* in the 16th century, women enjoyed prestigious positions in society. She was the priestess who held the community united. She was the medic and consoler of the soul. And language, before it was stunted, attested to the seeming equality of sexes. For instance, the word for rape was not known until the coming of the Spaniards. In fact, Sr. Mary John Mananzan, OSB, mentioned in a study that "a parish priest, Fr. Lorenzo Juan of Aringay, could categorically state that '*no existe la prostitucion en los pueblos idolatras.*'"

But the essentials of emancipated womanhood from priestess to presidency rest in the nebulosity of myths and condescensions. Centuries of foreign domination banished the position of equality between the sexes, until there were only traces in memories, legends and subjects for study and research.

The Spanish friars, for all the good things they contributed to the making of Philippine society, remain the culprit for the sad affairs of Filipino women today. Catholicism taught passivity and submissiveness as virtues and trademarks of being "good," particularly among women. To be aggressive is anathema and unbecoming for a girl, particularly so for a lady. Home-making and home economics are exclusively for the women to specialize. Education also is purposively taken to get a "good" husband. Once educated, to even attempt to transcend prescribed roles is to risk the ire of the general public and be called "a woman with balls."

At a time when poverty is not contaminating more than 70 percent of Philippine population, all's well in the women's front or, so it seemed, the women were at slumber. While history books cite exceptional women as among the country's revolutionary ancestors, the order of the day for women during the sixties was to be beautiful. American movies, American Top 40 music, and all-American goodies flooded the cultural sphere. Foreign domination in the economic and political fields was well-covered with sugar and spice. America was the Uncle Sam the country can depend on.

That was, however, the era before the First Quarter Storm of 1970. As student activism in the seventies reawakened a dormant nationalist fervor, it also unfolded in the process a militant women's organization. The MAKIBAKA (*Malayang Kilusan ng Bagong Kababaihan* or Free Movement of New Women) espoused not only a national democratic struggle but also the development of a women's consciousness. The movement was a milestone better than the suffragette movement of the early twenties, which was suspectedly used to the hilt by the conquering Americans in downplaying a rising nationalist sentiment that characterized the period.

The flowering of a genuine women's movement, however, was nipped in the bud with the declaration of Martial Law in 1972. MAKIBAKA was rendered illegal. The members were caught in the web and intricacies of building a revolutionary underground movement, setting aside the woman question.

The assassination of former Senator Benigno Aquino a decade later witnessed the mushrooming of various political organizations, including that of women. No longer the exclusive sphere of the middle class, women's organizations now encompass all classes and all political persuasions. Such organizations can be found among women workers, the urban poor, the religious, the middle class, women artists, peasants.

But the struggle to be counted in a male-dominated environment has a long way to go. A feudal mold and a strong "macho" culture threaten the development of a real women's movement.

The danger of imbibing an anti-male sentiment lies around the corner. An incursion of a patriarchal system plagues even the progressive circles. A number of women may find satisfaction, career and commitment-wise, by working with cause-oriented groups and organizations. Yet their role in the home front remains the same, albeit the presence of a "liberation husband."

As in the vernacular, the practice is "*sagad-sa-buto*" (bone-deep). The woman is still the General Manager in the kitchen; the Maintenance Engineer responsible for keeping the house spic and span; the Inventory Officer of socks, towels and wardrobe necessities. She is also the expected representative to various PTA (Parents-Teachers Association) meetings. She is responsible for countless other things that deaden creativity. She is the "accepted and expected" doer of things that do not count in the Gross National Product.

Schooling, for that matter, is not anymore only to catch a "good" husband, but more to earn a living. Schooling in most underdeveloped countries, for a fact, are not necessarily for education. After schooling there are those who find employment as secretaries, assistants, factory workers and other positions that receive low pay. The more skilled and more able professionals (men and women, for that matter) seek employment in other countries for better placement and pay. Setting aside humiliation, a good percentage of women with college degrees are now employed as domestic helpers and entertainers in countries like Hong Kong, Japan, Singapore, and in the Middle East and Europe.

Worse, a number of women sell themselves for prostitution and as brides to foreign nationals. Bright or tragic, these consequences are nonetheless essentially linked with the problems of poverty and the women's lack of opportunities to earn a decent living. Either as a courageous act or as an apathetic acceptance of a lifetime of sub-human existence, these women submit to these practices to escape or solve a structural injustice.

Poverty can either deaden or enlighten the consciousness of women. To an extent, poverty serves as a cathartic agent for women to go out and see the world for what it is. Economic necessity forces them to seek employment, and discover in the process that they are not welcome in a world men made for themselves. Indeed, what a way to be enlightened!

The condition of utter oppression, particularly of women, will usher in a thousand and one questions: Why the poverty? Why the structural injustice? Why are women not counted as equal members of society? Women must work doubly hard; they must be united to arrive at solutions to these problems. An irreversible evolution is the offing. And being a Christian nation has a lot to offer in the process of reawakening — both for women and men, interacting in building a better world where justice is perceived as justice, regardless of sex.

"... And She Said 'No' "

HELEN R. GRAHAM

In her book, *The Chalice and the Blade*, Riane Eisler states that feminism is the only ideology that frontally challenges the dominator model of human relations, as well as the principle of human ranking based on violence. When seen from the long view of cultural evolution, feminism is clearly not a new ideology. For millennia of cultural evolution, the idea of linking or partnership between human beings was operationally expressed in more equalitarian and peaceful societies, and this idea has surfaced, from time to time, throughout recorded history [1987:164f].

But the emergence of feminism as a modern ideology is traced to a convention held at Seneca Falls, New York in 1848 during which the women's struggle against subordination and degradation was formally launched. It was at that convention that Elizabeth Cady Stanton made the following pivotal statement: "Among the many important questions which have been brought before the public, there is none that more vitally affects the human family than that which is technically called 'women's rights'" [Eisler, ibid.].

Women in Asia, at the turn of the century, challenged by the rising aspirations of their peoples for national independence and autonomy, became "more conscious of their responsibility toward society and the bondage of patriarchy which weakened the nation by excluding the contribution of one-half of the people" [Kwok, 1989:95]. Women's participation in revolutionary and political activities, as Kwok Pui-lan notes, enabled them to explore new roles traditionally denied them [ibid.].

Our biblical heritage, which is marked by the androcentric and patriarchal character of the period of history in which it was produced, provides us with examples of how women coped with, maneuvered within or resisted the existing patriarchal culture. There is, for example, the story of the attractive widow, Judith, who made use of the tendency of patriarchal culture to see women only in terms of male sexual gratification. She was able to beguile the enemy general, Holofernes, and cut off his head. By thus forestalling the plan of the male elders to surrender [Judith 7:19-32], Judith brought liberation to her people [cf. c. 13].

There are also the stories of Rebekah [Genesis 27] and Tamar [Genesis 38], women who either circumvented or maneuvered within the patriarchal system. Rebekah secured the blessing of the first-born for Jacob, and Tamar forced Judah to admit that she was 'more just' than he [v. 26]. Ruth and Naomi, also functioning within the context of the patriarchal kinship framework, were able to empower each other to search together for personal well-being. In the process, Ruth and Naomi brought well-being to the entire village of Bethlehem, and ultimately, to the whole of Israel, since the son born of Ruth was destined to be the ancestor of David. For this, Ruth earned a place not only in the traditions of Israel, but she also appears as part of Matthew's genealogy of Jesus [1:5].

But none of these women directly confronted patriarchal culture, they simply coped, maneuvered and resisted from within the framework of the system.

One of the most delightful stories depicting women and patriarchy in the Bible is found in the book of Esther [c. 1]. It is the story of a non-Israelite woman, Queen Vashti, the wife of the Persian king, Ahasuerus. According to the story, King Ahasuerus, who 'reigned from India to Ethiopia' [v. 1] gave a banquet for all his bureaucrats and cronies, during which he showed off all 'the riches of his royal glory and the splendor and pomp of his majesty for... a hundred and eighty days' [v. 4]. When the king and his cronies were good and drunk, the king commanded that Queen Vashti be brought to appear before the drunken rabble in her royal regalia 'in order to show the peoples and the princes her beauty; for she was fair to behold' [v. 11]. But the queen said 'No' [cf. v. 12].

This unexpected challenge to his royal authority sent King Ahasuerus into a royal rage and he summoned his wise men to ascertain what the law prescribed with regard to Queen Vashti 'because she has not performed the command of King Ahasuerus' [1:15]. One can only imagine the consternation in the royal court. No one, let alone a woman, had ever said 'No' to the king! One of the wise men of the royal court, who knew the times, saw the grave consequences that this single 'No' might have for the entire structure of royal power. This is what he said to the king:

> Not only to the king has Queen Vashti done wrong, but also to all the princes and all the peoples who are in all the provinces of King Ahasuerus. For this deed of the queen will be made known to all women, causing them to look with contempt upon their husbands, since they will say, 'King Ahasuerus commanded Queen Vashti to be brought before him and she did not come.' This very day the ladies of Persia and Media who have heard of the queen's behavior will be telling it to all the king's princes, and there will be contempt and wrath in plenty [1:16b-18; emphasis added].

As Danna Fewell wryly comments with regard to this passage, "the action (or perhaps I should say non-action) of one woman threatens to collapse the entire structure of patriarchy in the entire Persian empire" [1987:83]. Queen Vashti must be dismissed before she 'infects' all the women of the empire! And so, a new queen was chosen from among 'all the beautiful virgins' gathered from all the provinces of the empire [2:2-4], and the structure of patriarchy was once again secure.

But a 'No' has been spoken, and women of both the Orient and the Occident are growing in the realization that the patriarchal dominance system has reached its logical limits. The dominator model extends beyond human social relations into the realm of non-human nature. The very survival of human life as we know it depends on our capacity to take an alternative route. The patriarchal dominance system is not the only option for human social relations, and for the relation of humans to the planet. Submerged cultural traditions from earlier periods, before the advent of patriarchy,

> reveal a long period of peace and prosperity when our social, technological, and cultural evolution moved upward; many thousands of years when all the basic technologies on which civilization is built were developed in societies that were not male dominant, violent, and hierarchic [Eisler, 1987:xvi].

We stand on the brink of a revolutionary cultural transformation of the scale of that which accompanied the shift from hunting-gathering and hunting-gardening societies to animal-plowed agriculture, urbanization and class societies, some seven to ten thousand years ago. If the planet and its inhabitants are to survive into the third millennium we — women and men — must all learn to say 'No' to the patriarchal establishments which threaten to close down all the basic life systems of our earth [cf. Berry, 1988:138-162].

The Church and the Woman Question

ROSE CERDEÑA-QUEBRAL

> "And God said: 'Let us make humanity in our image,' male
> and female God created them."
>
> — Genesis 1:26-27

The above passage states an eternal truth that human
beings have their dignity and worth rooted in the Creator
God who is the source of all life and, therefore, deserve to
live in community with fellow human beings.

The United Church of Christ in the Philippines (UCCP)
recently came up with a Statement of Faith. As a pastor,
I had the duty to expound to my local congregation what it
concretely means. The very first line reads: "We believe in
One God." In an Adult Sunday School class, I illustrated
this statement by drawing a circle above a line. There is one
God who alone is God, who is above all and yet chose to
dwell among the people. The people is represented by the

line which illustrates their being equal with one another. Any person or group of persons who put themselves above the line usurps God's throne, in a way declaring themselves as gods. Those who affirm their power and willingly submit to them are committing idolatry.

This truth is further illustrated by the teaching of Paul in his letter to the Galatian Christians when he wrote: "In Christ there is neither Jew nor Greek, neither slave nor free, neither male nor female." During the early years of Christianity our forebears fought long and hard whether or not to accept in their community of faith the non-Jews who became "Followers of the Way." One group insisted that non-Jews should first be circumcised before they can be accepted, implying that Jewishness was a prerequisite to Christianity and therefore being a Jew makes one superior. Another group insisted that as long as they believe that Jesus was the Christ, they are part of their community.

The second part of Paul's trilogy — "In Christ there is . . . neither slave nor free" — was tougher to deal with. It took white Christians more than 1,900 years to wrestle with this Christian imperative. For 1,900 years Christians owned slaves. Finally, after much struggle, they accepted that having slaves runs against the very grain of the faith they profess.

I believe that it is us, Christians of today, who are struggling with the third part of the trilogy: "In Christ there is . . . neither male nor female."

It is tempting to abuse the Scriptures and make it say what we want it to say. For instance, the story of The Fall for many people explains how evil came into the world, i.e., via the woman. In the story, after the first couple ate of the forbidden fruit, they hid themselves. God, walking in the garden, asked the man, "Did you eat of the fruit?" Then the man said, "It is the woman . . ." [*Genesis* 3:8-12] The phrase "it is the woman" is all that patriarchy needs to justify the subjugation of women. The word of the man is accepted as eternal truth without dealing with the real message of the story. For the story reveals the human tendency not to take responsibility for one's sin. At that moment humanity's oneness, as represented by the man and the woman living together in fellowship, respect, freedom and equality, was broken because man dominated woman by making her take sole responsibility for their disobedience. Perhaps the man even thought that God would join him in damning the woman. But we all know this did not happen because both received the justice and mercy of God.

Even liturgy is being used to justify patriarchy. In the local church where I serve, there was quite a reaction from the congregation when I officiated a wedding for the first time. I changed some parts of the ritual to make the ceremony more in keeping with our faith in a liberating God, expressed in liberating relationships. Instead of just the father walking with the bride, both bride and groom march with their parents along the aisle. The veil, which was traditionally put over the groom's shoulder and over the bride's head, is put over both their heads to symbolize the couple's mutual submission to the Holy Spirit's guidance, or over both their shoulders to symbolize their partnership and equality in the responsibility for the relationship. The coins, instead of being given by the groom to the bride, are given by the minister to both bride and groom as symbols of God's provision and of their role as stewards in sharing God's blessings with everyone. I dared to make these changes because I believe that church rituals must be faithful to the concrete realities of life for it to be meaningful, for it to be significant. We recognize that human relationships are a major factor in human liberation; and this should be expressed in our liturgy.

Last Easter, in April 1988, during the launching of the Ecumenical Decade of the Churches in Solidarity with Women by the National Council of Churches in the Philippines, I spoke about liberating our liturgy by challenging our churches in the use of inclusive language in our songs, prayers and homilies. Most of those who attended were women and two clergymen. Clergymen from other NCCP member churches were visibly absent. Their poor attendance seems to indicate that the vast majority of the clergy, largely male, still cannot bring themselves to accept women as equal partners in the ministry.

Humanity's oneness was broken because man dominated woman

A case in point is a convention I attended. The convention was dominated by men: all the officers, most of the staff (except for the kitchen crew), and the delegates were mostly men. The only women were the women's association representative and three or four other female delegates out of more than fifty delegates. It was not surprising therefore that during the election of new officers for the next biennium, all the nominees were men. It is beyond my understanding how our church's Constitution can provide for a youth representative out of eight delegates per conference while not mandating at least one female representative per conference. Most conferences, therefore, end up with eight male representatives. This is absurd especially when majority of our constituency are women. Albeit delayed, I believe a constitutional amendment should correct this injustice within the church's structure.

I was inspired by a Bible study given by Bishop Benito Dominguez where he drew lessons from women characters in the Bible. He mentioned how Jesus affirmed Mary [*Luke* 10:38-42] because Mary did not allow herself to be put in a box or in a stereotype role. He said that the challenge for the church is to be like Mary — full of surprises and not limited by what society expects. The church must also have the vision of the woman who anointed Jesus' feet [*Luke* 7:36-50], of the woman who could accept the sacrifices and pain that Jesus had to go through in the process of giving birth to a new creation. The church, to be able to fully celebrate, must be ready to participate as co-creators with God. During our discussion I suggested that as church leaders witnessing to our constituents, we should "fix our ranks" and accept women as full partners in the ministry. I asked the group of male pastors: "Can we accept that any kind of dominion is a sign of The Fall? Can we accept that the superiority of the male over the female is a myth?" Pandemonium broke loose in the ensuing discussion. Somehow I got the sad answer to my question: church leaders are not ready for this partnership. I realized that men must be liberated from their fragile egos, and women from their powerlessness.

It is true that in the midst and in the context of an increasingly oppressive and exploitative society, the Philippine church is challenged more than ever to examine the bedrock of its mission. The church can never rest with the growing restlessness of the basic masses and marginalized sectors of society. The theme of the UCCP Convention, "The Church in the Struggle for the Life of the World," implies that the church must be where the action is: in the struggle of the peasants for genuine land reform; in the struggle of small fisherfolk for the equal sharing of marine resources; in the struggle of workers for decent wages; in the struggle of students for a democratic and nationalist education; in the struggle of the urban poor for a humane life; in the struggle of tribal communities for their ancestral lands; in the struggle of women against patriarchy; even in the struggle of church workers against harassment and persecution. The church is called upon to expose and oppose all forms of power that oppress and exploit others.

The church, to be the church of Christ, is called upon to do a lot to realize the reign of the sovereign God. But how can God's reign come when even as we struggle, women who represent at least half of humanity remain trivialized, unrecognized, powerless and dehumanized? Can we be truly victorious in claiming social change when the woman question remains unresolved? We who acknowledge the need for a holistic salvation must realize that no one is truly free until **all** are free. No one can be safe and secure until the righteousness of God prevails. No one can experience fullness of life until all are experiencing it. For we are a community. We are one body, parts of one another. No, no man is free until women are free. The pain of women is the pain of God. Or don't we realize that part of God is woman too?

Rural Women in thePhilippines:

Some Notes on their Current Status and Problems

CAROLYN ISRAEL-SOBRITCHEA

The Philippines is basically an agrarian society with a semi-feudal and semi-colonial social formation. About 70 percent of its 50 million population is in the agricultural sector and is dependent on it for economic survival. The semi-feudal character of the country underscores peasant labor as among the most important factors of production. Many local studies more than adequately articulate the status and conditions of life of the Filipino peasants in general. However, practically very little is being done in terms of analyzing the specific conditions and problems of peasant women in the Philippines.

This paper addresses this concern. It presents a brief overview of the demographic profile of Filipino peasant women today and their role in the household and community. It also discusses the factors constraining their wider participation in productive activity and the improvement of their overall condition in life.

About two-thirds of the 24 million Filipino women today live in the rural areas. Most of them are wives and daughters of agricultural workers and therefore are part of the majority of Filipinos who live on predominantly subsistence existence.

Statistics portray that rural females come from families with an average size of six and an annual income of P4,715.00 (1975). From a rural mother's standpoint, this means feeding and clothing each household member for a little more than two pesos daily.

Some 90 percent of rural females are literate by government standards. Such a seemingly impressive figure does not mean much to these women who barely have the necessary skills for the job market. Only a few rural women finish secondary schooling and fewer still go college.

In terms of age distribution, only one-third of the female population in rural areas are above 15 years of age. This implies that most village women are still growing children whose life concerns are almost the same as their elders.

Statistics also indicate that although the life expectancy of rural women (63 years) may be a little higher than their counterparts in other developing countries, they are no different from them who go through life in abject poverty, managing meager home resources, and attending to often malnourished children while they themselves suffer from periodic bouts of nutritional deficiency. The married Filipino woman may occasionally lose a child to pneumonia or gastroenteritis, two of leading causes of infant mortality in the countryside today. In more unfortunate cases, the mother herself may die prematurely from pregnancy or childbirth-related disorder due to lack of adequate and immediate medical attention.

Unlike their more economically privileged urban neighbors, rural women are mostly preoccupied with the day-to-day concerns of survival. Because of necessity rather than choice, they are active members of the labor force, a role that does not come easy when one is barely out of childhood or when one is a wife, mother and housekeeper all at the same time.

Rural Women in the Labor Force

National figures show that housekeeping is the most significant activity of women in this country. Rural-urban comparisons tend to reflect that more village women spend the major part of their lives as full-time housekeepers. While only three percent of all rural women 15 years old and over are listed in Government records as unemployed, 53 percent of them are not at all included part of the labor force. These figures are, of course, misleading since they do not account for many non-income generating but nonetheless economically productive activities of women.

Female labor forms the major part of unpaid family labor in the countryside. This includes assistance provided by a farmer's wife and daughters in such activities as food preparation for hired workers, seedbed preparation, or purchase of farm equipment and supplies. It also includes the production of household needs that would otherwise be bought in the market.

In addition to work that falls under the classification "family labor," rural women have a sizeable share of the manpower input for contractual labor, particularly in agriculture. A study published in 1980 by the National Commission on the Role of Filipino Women (NCRFW) shows that 36 percent of hired labor involving all phases of farm operations come from women. Their contribution is highest in planting (49 percent), harvesting (48 percent), tilling (46 percent) and threshing (44 percent).

Outside of crop farming, many rural women are engaged in backyard cultivation of vegetables for home consumption or for the market; raising poultry or livestock; operation of *sari-sari* (variety) store; or domestic service for rich households in nearby towns or cities. Depending on the dominant industry in the community, they also engage in weaving of mats and hats, pottery-making, or production of local delicacies. Many of these occupations, done intermittently and on part-time basis, often escape official monitoring.

On the whole, the majority of employed rural women are in farming while the rest are in sales, production process work, and service-oriented occupations. In contrast, urban women workers are mostly in sales and service occupations while only a handful occupy professional and technical positions.

Considering the active participation of rural women in the labor force, one may readily presume that they are at par with men in terms of relative contribution to the national income. Unfortunately, there is a wide disparity in income between them. The same study of the NCRFW indicates that while the average weekly earnings of male and female workers increased over the past years, the latter's income was on the average lower than that of male workers.

This disparity is most evident in agriculture where the women's average weekly income in 1977 was slightly lower, one-third of 29.2 percent, than that of the men. In rice production, for example, female workers were paid from 30 centavos to more than two pesos lower in their daily wage for all types of farm operations except harvesting compared to male workers. On the national scale, the Commission estimates that for every peso paid to a Filipino worker, only 35 percent goes to the female worker.

The relatively low income received by Filipino women as a whole may be the result of the sex-linked nature of many occupations and of the generally low regard, economically speaking, toward many female-dominated jobs. It is interesting to note that while there is no significant difference in literacy rates nor enrolment figures in all levels of education between men and women, men tend to dominate higher paying jobs. Thus, women can be found among the so-called "rank and file" in provincial and municipal government and private offices. The others become teachers or sales clerks and market vendors.

The disparity both in allocation of jobs and income between sexes is often explained in terms of the varying requirements of occupations. The common argument is that certain jobs are more physically demanding and risky and therefore require male labor. Another argument claims men to be more efficient workers since they are not saddled by child-rearing and housekeeping roles. Such arguments provide a very simplistic view of the situation and lack a deeper understanding of the social conditions that perpetuate work practices discriminatory to women.

Rural Women and their Traditional Roles

The popular belief that Filipino women go out to work only when home conditions allow does not seem to hold true among many poor rural women. While it is true that many Filipinos, men and women alike, still regard homemaking as the most ideal lifetime activity of married women, the increasing number of them in the labor force indicates that such an ideal is becoming more and more difficult to realize.

As Illo points out in her study on "Constraints to Rural Women's Participation in Philippine Development" (1979), poorer women are less bound by the norm to give priority to household responsibilities since their overriding concern is the family's survival. What appears to be more important for them, therefore, is to work whenever work is available and to catch up with domestic chores at the end of the day once the job is over. This arrangement is more possible in the rural areas since most occupations women are able to get are seasonal and short-term.

It should be expected that once a woman shares in the burden of earning a living, her traditional roles in the family are correspondingly shared with, if not relegated to, other family members. Otherwise, how is it possible for her to reconcile the competing demands of work and home? Ethnographic and sociological studies are rife with accounts of how rural women cope with their multiple roles.

In most of these accounts, it is the existence of certain cultural forms — particularly the functional extended family system, close neighborhood relations, and "surrogate motherhood" — which allow working mothers to work and manage the home at the same time. Elder children are particularly helpful as secondary housekeepers in many rural households. The same holds true for rural husbands, although their share of household chores is not as significant as can be expected. This is in view of the highly sex-

oriented patterns of socialization which hardly prepare men to assume a more active domestic role.

Ethnographic studies of various lowland cultural communities point to the "equalitarian" character of man-woman relations (e.g., Fox, 1958; Anderson, 1962; Sheans, 1976). Fox, for instance, asserts that the Filipino family is neither patriarchal nor matriarchal; that on the contrary, Filipino men and women share the exercise of power and authority especially in the household. Such situation is attributed to the nature of the bilateral kinship structures. Fox adds that "though marriage forms the 'new family of procreation,' the husband and wife are still an integral part of their respective families of orientation. If the husband abuses his wife, for example, her kinsmen will intervene for she is still a member of her natal group."

Other ethnographies claim that the better status of Filipino peasant women compared to their Asian counterparts is due to the former's active participation in economic activity and prevailing rules of marital residence and inheritance. The patterns of marital residence in Philippine society vary usually on account of such pragmatic considerations as place of employment or the availability *per se* of a place to live. Residing in the man's locality is not an ideal pattern and, in fact, is resorted to only when the couple derives some economic and other benefits from doing so.

The prevailing pattern of inheritance in many cultural communities in the country does not discriminate against women. Children, regardless of sex and age, share in inheritance. There are, however, occasional preference for the eldest and youngest and for the males when inheritance involves real property. In some cases, as among the Suban Ilocanos, Sheans notes that properties acquired by gift and inheritance are owned individually. He adds that both husband and wife "may have full rights in separate estates from which their spouses are barred" and both dispose of each one's property as they see fit.

While the aforementioned data somehow point to a more favorable solution to the problems of Filipino peasant women, serious questions can be raised about the validity of such observations. It is a known fact, for example, that the so-called equalitarian relationship between men and women does not go beyond the household and kinship units and does not reflect on various aspects of community life. In most cases, peasant women hardly participate in community-wide decision-making processes. Men tend to dominate positions at all levels of the political structure and control the flow and extent of all aspects of farm work.

More Problems and Challenges

Some recent developments in the countryside do not seem to augur well for rural women. Changing structures in the agricultural economy, including population pressure and technological innovations, seem to make things worse for them. Unemployment is highest in their group as a result of lack of new job opportunities and the disappearance of old ones. The introduction of mechanical harvesters and threshers, for instance, is displacing a lot of women workers. So is the conversion of tracts of rice and corn fields into residential lots or fields for commercial crop cultivation that are less dependent on female labor.

Community organizers decry the Government's lack of emphasis on developing economically productive skills and knowhow for women. Some argue that measures to improve the production of rice and corn farming will go a long way toward raising the status of the female labor force. Still, most agricultural programs are geared toward the males, with females relegated to home economics and family planning programs. Farm innovations are generally addressed to men, although a substantial portion of the work in the field is done by women. While women participate actively in making decisions affecting the farm and take charge of backyard gardening and livestock-raising, they never become deliberate beneficiaries of rural development programs.

What seems to be most revealing is the rural woman's minimal participation in political affairs. Neher's (1980) study of Cebuano women underscores this situation. The Cebuano women strongly resist involvement in local politics not only because of cultural reasons but also because of a high degree of alienation and lack of confidence in their own political efficacy. They share with their men a strong sense of cynicism. This, however, hardly translates into positive action which involves, for example, a stronger articulation of their problems and needs and a changing of the conditions that foster such attitudes which limit their participation in political affairs.

Many rural organizations are coming about lately, but none seem to underscore the peculiarities and problems of peasant women. An approach such as this, if undertaken, could hasten the improvement of women's status in the rural areas and draw them faster into the mainspring of national life.

Women in the Cordilleras

CAROL GAMIAO

The recent history of the Central Cordilleras abound with unforgettable anecdotes of how women actively participated in the people's resistance against capitalist incursion, government-imposed development, and militarization.

In 1978, Kalinga mothers in Tinglayan, Kalinga-Apayao literally pulled out their youthful sons from a detachment of the Philippine Constabulary where they were detained following the counter-insurgency drive in the village. Earlier, the Bontoc women of Mainit successfully resisted the entry of Benguet Corporation, one of the country's top mining concerns.

The women of Suyo in Sagada, Mountain Province demanded direct participation in the *ator*, the council of elders in Bontoc society. This case, however, is more an exception than the rule throughout the region. The active participation of women in the defense of their ancestral land did not confer to them a status equal to men.

The situation in the Cordilleras remains much like elsewhere in the country where women can justly claim to be victims of national, class and gender oppression. A review of the situation of women in other sectors in the region indicates the nature of women's problems that needs to be addressed.

THE SITUATION OF CORDILLERA WOMEN

Traditional women

There are indicators from historical sources that pre-colonial women held a position equal to men. Unfortunately, the Cordilleras, which was able to resist colonization and retain many of its socio-political institutions, is by no means a living example of such an ideal state of affairs.

Cordillera women do play special roles in the ritual life of the community. The *manjajawak* (healer) of Kalinga, for instance, is a woman. In agriculture, women are called upon to perform the necessary rituals before the planting season can commence.

On the whole, however, men dominate indigenous political structures like the *bodong* (peace pact) and the *ator* (council of elders). While certain means exist allowing women to have their say in certain deliberations in the *ator*, direct women's participation in community decision-making is not institutionalized. In fact, it is taboo for women to set foot on the *ator*.

Women in agriculture

Traditionally, Cordillera societies are warrior societies. The present system in agricultural production is a carry-over of the division of labor characteristic of such a set-up. As the men go to war to defend the territorial boundaries of their villages, women are left to take care of food production and to look after the children.

To this day, food production remains primarily a woman's domain. In paddy rice production, the men are charged with field preparation; thereafter, farm activities rest on women. Where there are swidden farms, it is the women who trek the mountains to maintain the gardens and to collect the produce. At the same time, it is also their duty to augment meager farm production with other livelihood activities like swine and poultry raising.

In areas where feudal structures are established, such as the vegetable industry in Benguet, gender and class oppression become evident as women and child laborers are paid lower than men. While both men and women are given similar work, the male *oblante* or worker is paid P40 a day while the female worker gets only P25 (1987 rates).

In the big landholdings of lowland Kalinga and Ifugao, the oppressive tenancy conditions weigh more heavily on the women than they do on the men. As a salve to chronic indebtedness to the landlord, the women in the household take on menial jobs like washing, cleaning and other odd jobs in exchange for food and used clothing.

Women workers

The women in the labor force should be better off. However, the growth of the industrial sector, with the presence of an Export Processing Zone (EPZ) in Baguio, shows that workers almost everywhere share similar conditions. The Baguio EPZ employs about 4,500 people, 86 percent of whom are women. Here, the classic methods of exploitation of female workers are all in use. Union-busting, sexual harassment, absence of security of tenure, poor working conditions all prove to be detrimental to the health and reproductive functions of women.

Whereas many unemployed and underemployed residents and migrants see the EPZ as instrumental in bringing in jobs to the city, statistics show that the real beneficiaries in the past years are the 10 companies of the

Baguio EPZ. These companies garnered the highest production among all EPZs, topping even that of Bataan's over 40 firms. In 1986, the workers' share of profit was only 0.3 percent of total production compared to the 15 percent in Bataan.

In the absence of industries in the countryside, women are forced to migrate to the urban centers to search for jobs in multinational companies or in lucrative export-oriented enterprises. Most of the piece-workers in these enterprises, for example, are Bontoc, Kankanay and Ifugao weavers. While the owners earn a lot of dollars from their produce, these women workers are often overworked, underpaid, and without the legal benefits of employment.

Urban poor

The urban poor community now swells to an estimated 60 percent of the population of Baguio City, the only urban center in the Cordilleras. This increase reflects the absence of job opportunities and the increasing economic pressures in the migrants' highland communities of origin.

Expectant but unable to find better living conditions in the city, urban poor women display coping mechanisms while appropriating for themselves jobs that nobody else would take — buying and selling used bottles and old newspapers, fetching water, sidewalk vending, and others. Because they live in what are considered squatter areas, they do not enjoy the full benefits of available city services and thus face the constant fear of dislocation.

Women professionals

Statistics reveal that more Cordillera women are now able to finish college degrees. This is important in terms of articulating the demands of women in the Cordilleras. However, because of the conservative content of the educational program, only a few women are leading politically active lives. Others are yet to liberate themselves from chauvinistic husbands who expect them to manage career and home at the same time with very little support.

Militarization

Increasing militarization in many parts of the region is certainly one aspect of Cordillera life affecting the situation of women. The Cordillera is highly militarized supposedly to counter the growing resistance of the people against the exploitation of the land's natural resources such as minerals, timber, hydroelectric power, and others.

The intensifying conflict between military troops and rebel forces affect hapless civilians, especially those in the countryside. Whole communities are dislocated due to military operations.

Under these deteriorating conditions, women bear the trauma of seeing their husbands or children being detained or killed, while at the same time functioning as sole providers for their families.

There are also many documented cases of innocent women and children becoming direct victims of violence in Kalinga-Apayao. Crimes against women such as rape are also recorded. In addition, prostitution, which was unheard of before in these areas, occur in heavy concentration among soldiers.

WOMEN'S RESPONSE

Involvement in so-called women's concerns is a recent phenomenon among the indigenous women of the Cordilleras who often have their minds full of the daily problems of survival. Many women's organizations existing in the region, however, are conservative and not liberating. Their political orientation becomes apparent during electoral contests among factions in the ruling elite.

The first militant women's organization in the Cordilleras emerged from the urban labor sector in 1985. The *Kilusan ng mga Manggagawang Kababaihan* (KMK), or Women

Workers Movement, took root in the Baguio Export Processing Zone.

Then in 1986, the Cordillera Women's Education and
Resource Center (CWERC) was established following a
Cordillera-wide consultation among women. The center
was formed to assist in setting up a women's movement in
the Cordilleras that is well-grounded on the particularities
of the woman question in the region and on the national
character of women's oppression in general. Formerly as
the Baguio-Benguet Women's Education and Resource
Center, it was able to make significant strides in organizing
women students, women professionals, and urban poor
women.

The CWERC envisions a women's movement for the
Cordilleras that proceeds from the need for women to
liberate themselves from cultural restrictions that hamper
the attainment of their full potentials as individuals. It
affirms at the same time that the women's struggle against
oppression cannot be dissociated from the nationwide
struggle against the exploitative structures in Philippine
society. After all, women are those who are more often left
to bear the brunt of hard times and, in the process,
invariably experience male bias. Indeed, poverty and
gender discrimination are two sides of institutionalized
violence under an unjust set-up.

The experience of the church-based Social Action
Center teaches a valuable lesson in organizing among
women. The Center's Women's Program attempted to
organize the women workers of Tiong San Bazaar, a
Chinese-owned department store and the largest in Baguio
City.

The Program failed to encourage analysis of the different
contradictions in society which relate to their problems as
women. Lacking this perspective, the union was weak from
the very start. The attempt ended in the dismissal of the
women workers, and the Women's Program folded up
eventually.

In the pursuit of change, women must understand that they cannot win freedom from the structures of dominance if they fail to link their particular struggle with the national struggle of the entire Filipino people. It is well to realize that the female population must be mobilized to advance its concerns and aspirations within an overall liberationist framework.

Given the situation in the Cordillera and throughout the country today, the side that this half of the population will take will be decisive in shifting the balance of forces towards a more desirable social order where women are the equals of men in a just and democratic society.

The Miner's Wife

Victoria Corpuz, Evangeline Ram and Cynthia Dacanay

Most researches done on the mining industry give comprehensive and extensive data on the exploitation of mine workers and the industry's destructive effects on ecology. However, there is seldom attention given to the miserable condition of women in the mines, more specifically, the miners' wives.

Antamok Mine is the oldest mine site of Benguet Corporation (formerly the Benguet Consolidated Incorporated). The Mine started its operations in 1903 and, until recently, concentrated its activities in the extraction of high-grade ore from the underground. At present, a large portion of its ore extracts is generated from open-pit mining.

Antamok is also the oldest and biggest gold-producing mine in the region. It accounts for a large percentage of the total gross production of gold in 1987 when Benguet Gold

Operations alone produced 1,224,536,000 pesos in gold. This mining company is known to be controlled by big foreign capitalists who use Filipino nationals as dummies to safeguard their interests.

The company makes use of subtle manipulation and deception in recruiting its workers: it promises free housing, free water and electricity, and other benefits. The workers then would expect to enjoy decent living and working conditions and to receive high wages. However, actual conditions in the mining community show that the company does not keep its promises.

The Mining Community

Approximately 2,000 workers are presently employed in the Antamok Mine. The total population in the community is 6,000, with families coming from different ethnolinguistic groups, majority of whom are from the Cordillera region.

The workers and their families live in bunkhouses located within the perimeter of the mining company. The bunkhouses were constructed as early as the 1930s so that the original fixtures for water and sewage remain up to this day. At present, there are 37 bunkhouses. A bunkhouse accommodates 40 to 50 families, with an average of seven persons per family.

The camp has an old elementary school building which caters to the schooling of the workers' younger children, while some eight kilometers from the mine is a private Catholic high school. There is also a public school within the camp which caters mostly to children in the nearby communities.

There is a dispensary run by two resident doctors, a library with dilapidated and obsolete books, an old bowling alley, a cinema, a Catholic church and an Iglesia Ni Kristo church. Several small stores are also rented out by the company to enterprising residents in addition to the concessions.

The Bunkhouse

A typical family in the bunkhouse is provided with a room measuring 8 feet by 15 feet. This room is multi-purpose: as bedroom, living room, dining room and kitchen all at once. A thin galvanized iron sheet or plywood separates the rooms in the bunkhouse. One feature of bunkhouse life is the lack, even absence, of privacy within and among the families. As one woman described it, even the "creaking of the bed" cannot escape the ears of one's next door neighbor. No private affair remains secret for long, for in a short time, it becomes public knowledge, making privacy a luxury.

Another feature of bunkhouse life is the communal use of bathrooms, washrooms and comfort rooms making health and sanitation a major problem. This condition is complicated by inadequate water supply that worsens during the dry season. The lack of water accounts for the stink and filth pervasive in the comfort rooms and surrounding environs. There is inadequate water supply because the company supplies water for the underground tunnel first.

The mine residents also complain of the water's brownish color and the residue it leaves in water containers. Most of the water pipes are old, dilapidated and leaking most of the time, besides being close to the sewage pipes which are in a similar state. The company also cautions the people to boil first their drinking water for 10 minutes which only proves that the tap water is unsafe for human consumption.

The Woman in the Mines

A miner and his family must learn to live with deplorable conditions in the mines. The woman struggles with these conditions 24 hours a day. While the miner contends with difficult working conditions in the underground tunnel, the woman wages her struggle within the confines of her home and community. While the miner is burdened with the responsibility of providing for the financial needs of his family, the woman is burdened with budgeting her husband's meager salary in addition to housework and childcare. On top of this, she confronts daily the miserable environment in the mining community.

As a wife, the woman in the mines must adjust her schedule in relation to her husband's work shift. Whichever shift he is in, she must always be there to send him off and meet him when he comes home. She is expected to accommodate whatever his needs are. Having sex, whenever the husband so desires, is a pressure the woman learns to live with. On Sundays or between shifts, the miner usually brings over his friends to drink, and the woman is expected to serve them and tolerate their drinking session even when there is only one room for everyone to occupy.

There is virtually no opportunity for a married couple to cultivate richer and closer emotional intimacy. The condition in the mines lacks privacy and limits the woman's relationship with her husband only to her housewifely chores and to physical intimacy. Cases of wife-beating in the bunkhouses are taken matter-of-factly. When the husband is in a violent temper or when he is irritable, it is considered natural that he takes this out on his wife. Even then, the woman does not perceive this as a loss of love on her husband's side. In some cases, she would even blame herself for the beatings she gets.

As a mother, her foremost responsibility is to take care of her children and ensure their well-being. However, the conditions that would permit her to provide a healthy environment for the growth and development of her children is absent. The meager salary of her husband prevents her from buying nutritious food. The unsanitary surroundings expose her children to diseases such as dysentery and other stomach disorders. Her personal needs always come after she takes care of the needs of her family.

As a housekeeper, she attends to the cleaning of the house, the washing and ironing of clothes, and such other

chores that need to be done for the maintenance of her home. These chores are complicated by the inadequate water supply and poor facilities in the bunkhouse. For instance, she uses a great deal of time queuing up for water.

Budgeting a weekly salary of 426 pesos ($20.00) for a family of six is a tough job, considering that the current poverty threshold is 1,134 pesos per week. The housewife is thus compelled to look for other sources of income. She may borrow money at usurious rates, or get goods in advance with prices 50 to 60 percent higher than the normal buying price. Even if she is able to pay her debts regularly (which is not often the case), new accounts are continually incurred. She may engage in income-generating projects like hog or chicken-raising, selling, sewing or weaving. She may also work as "food handler," which is quite taxing because of stiff requirements set by the company. Some women may also engage in private mining, or let their children do odd jobs for minimal fees. There are some company-sponsored projects for women such as weaving, doll-making and crocheting. But these do not appeal to them because the piece rate system of paying their services is too low.

Burdened by domestic tasks and the emotional stresses of being wife and mother and managing a household on meager income, the woman in the mines generally feels a lingering frustration about her daily existence. Not only is she physically exhausted, she is also continuously under psychological stress. Her agony is aggravated by the absence of meaningful and challenging activities. Despite her frustrations, the miner's wife prevails over her situation and somehow succeeds in making a home for her husband and children.

She learns to withstand the pressures and demands of mine life and, in the process, develops a good sense of humor, a high level of frustration tolerance, level-headedness, and a drive to make her life and that of her family better. The misery of living in the mine does not discourage her. Instead, it becomes a challenge that drives her to seek alternatives. These are the positive qualities of the women in the mines which gave birth to the women's organization in the mining community.

The Women's Organization

The full potential of the local labor union in the mines, one of the more militant unions in the area, was at first hindered by the lack of support from the women. The women at that time perceived the strikes and other militant actions of the miners as pointless. There were a few women, however, who realized that the problems they confront within the confines of their homes are linked with the problems in the entire mining community. In 1985, these women organized themselves and later on drew in more women into their activities.

At the beginning, the efforts of these women were met with indifference and sarcasm. Earlier attempts in organizing women failed to address the peculiar needs and characteristics of women in the mines. Then in January 1988, the Antamok Women's Organization was formed. It carried a nationalist orientation. The organization grew and, with the increase in the women's level of political consciousness, became a strong force in forwarding the demands of mine workers. They are now actively supporting political rallies and strikes. In some instances, they directly engaged in protest activities demanding immediate action to their bunkhouse problems.

There is a women's organization initiated by the mining company to attend to bunkhouse problems. This organization, however, is powerless because its moves are largely dictated by the company. It causes division within the labor union because the company used the women members to discourage miners from joining protest actions.

The Antamok Women's Organization was formed through the initiative of the women themselves. It seeks to empower women and develop their potential to become a potent force in the people's movement in the mining community. It stands on the principle that their struggle as women in the mining community, though distinct, is vital and integral to the struggle of mine workers in the community.

The whole setup in the mining industry is a microcosm of the semi-feudal, semi-colonial and patriarchal system that pervades the entire Philippine society. This system sustains itself by continuously and indiscriminately exploiting mine workers and their families. The decent wage and proper living and working conditions that are denied the workers enable the mining company to amass huge profits. It aggravates the oppression of women by denying them a more humane and decent environment that could ensure their own well-being and that of the present and reserved labor force. The gross neglect of women through sub-human living conditions is unjust and exploitative. It is in this context that a strong and militant women's movement is conceived to work hand in hand with the worker's movement, not only to advance the workers' demands but also to address the particular needs and concerns of women.

June 1988

Do Prostitutes Have Human Rights?

Brenda Stoltzfus

> *"I look happy on the outside but inside I am always crying."*

> *"What I want for my life is work that gives me enough to live on and to send my children to school. I don't want to be rich . . . just to have enough."*

> *"The reason American men like Filipinas is because we are cheap."*
> — "hospitality women" in Olongapo

Women working in the "rest and recreation industry" around the United States military bases in the Philippines are commonly called *prostitutes*. Those of us who work directly with these women, however, choose to call them *prostituted women*. It is not true that they chose to be prostitutes, that they like their work, and that they make a lot of money. What they say (as in the above quotes) belie these myths. The reality within which these women are trapped can be called *institutionalized rape*.

Women end up in the bars and clubs of Olongapo and Angeles (the cities outside American bases Clark and Subic) largely due to poverty and the discrimination they experience as women. They find themselves in a situation where wealthy bar owners make large profits from selling women's bodies to US servicemen who are free to buy women for a "good time." Researches done on war and conquering armies throughout history (e.g., Susan Brownmiller) reveal that soldiers rape the women of the country they are conquering. The US institutionalized this type of rape in the Philippines. As hospitality women in Olongapo point out, the US servicemen like the Philippines because its women are cheap.

Prostitution is usually understood in two ways: one, that it is a moral problem and therefore the women are sinners; or, that it is a problem stemming from unjust structures and therefore the women are victims. The first, I contend, is a classic example of blaming the victim as in the case of women who are raped.

Inday is a typical example of women in Olongapo. She came to Manila from Samar to work as a maid when she was about fourteen or fifteen years old. She got married but later left her husband when he started to continually beat her and their children. She ended up in Olongapo because, with an elementary level education, she could not find work that paid enough to support herself and her three children. She now has a fourth child from an American soldier from whom she receives no financial support.

In the bar where she works, which is owned by an American, Inday does not have a right to refuse invitations from customers. If she refuses, the bar fine (equivalent to the amount the customer pays to take her out, and from which she receives a commission) will be charged to her. If she accepts but later on the customer is not satisfied, he

can ask for his money back and the bar fine will still be charged to her. She does not receive a regular salary and depends only on commissions. She earns only when a ship is in port. During extended periods when no ships dock at the port, she may need to loan money to feed herself and the child who stays with her. Whenever possible, she sends money back home to her family where her other children are staying.

There are thousands of women like Inday. Her story speaks further to break the myths and stereotypes around prostitution. One must ask, did Inday have human rights now as a woman working in a club?

Prostituted women are marginalized and ostracized in society. As such, they are seen as people not in a position to assert their human rights unless they leave their work. Leaving the prostitution industry is, however, not a simple matter of making a decision for them. Majority of them will not be able to leave their work unless major economic and political changes take place in the country; unless the bases are removed; unless there is genuine land reform in the provinces; and unless the women's movement is taken seriously.

The moral issues raised concerning the problem of prostitution are perhaps focused in the wrong context. Prostitution around the American bases is a manifestation of larger problems. Some questions perhaps need to be asked to focus our sight on this problem: What right do wealthy bar owners have to sell women's bodies for larger profits? What right does the US have to retain their bases on Philippine soil and to interfere in Philippine economic and political affairs? Who is morally to blame for the social problems in the bases areas? Who is the human rights violator?

Women and
their Experience of
Human Rights Violations

From Inside Prison Walls

Elisa Tita Lubi

Female prisoners are the most common victims of sexual harassment, molestation and rape. While these acts are also committed against male prisoners, the rate of incidence is much higher among women.

Even before a woman detainee is brought to prison, chances are, she is already manhandled, touched or caressed by those who arrested her. This continues up to the period of interrogation and investigation. At the police precinct, a male police officer would sometimes take it upon himself to strip search the female detainee even though regulations state that only female police officers can conduct strip searches on female prisoners. To most young and good-looking female prisoners, there would also be innuendoes, suggestive talk, and even sexual advances in exchange for freedom.

Sexual molestation or rape is the most common form of torture during tactical interrogation of female political prisoners. Age or appearance does not matter because sexual molestation serves a purpose apart from mere sexual pleasure. It is intended to force the detainee to divulge information that would, for instance, lead to the arrest of her associates who are also wanted by the military or police. This sexual harassment could continue throughout the duration of incarceration. There would be overt gestures of sexual abuse such as fondling and caressing, actual seduction and acts of lasciviousness against the female prisoner.

Courting a female prisoner is common practice for a jailguard. He would promise better treatment hoping that this would force her to give in to his sexual advances. If the female prisoner is much older than the jailguard, he would turn to her young daughter who is "offered" the chance to insure better prison treatment for her mother. The female prisoner, or the daughter in the latter case, is more likely to accept such offers not only to get special treatment but, most of the time, out of fear that rejection might only increase the hardships she, or the daughter's mother, is already undergoing inside prison. The higher the rank of the "suitor," the more difficult it is for her to refuse.

Here is my own story:

> When they brought me blindfolded to an undisclosed place and sat me down on a backless sofa, it suddenly hit me that I was going to be tortured. A sense of resignation and acceptance of my fate enveloped my consciousness. I thought, well, it seems I won't be able to escape torture after all. Together with this thought came my resolve to bravely take without succumbing whatever would be inflicted on me. No matter what would happen, they can never make me divulge any information they wanted from me.

They opened my blouse and started fondling me. Questions started pouring in. When I refused to answer the questions without the presence of my lawyer, they went on to undress me completely. They continued to fondle me and touch me in my private parts while whispering obscenities in my ear. When they still could not get the information they wanted, they proceeded to do worse things on my body. The molestation was terrible. They said they would insert red pepper, bottles and electrodes in my vagina. They would rape me, they threatened.

I insisted on invoking my constitutional right against self-incrimination and to remain silent in the absence of counsel. Finally, they asked me if I really didn't want to say anything. I shook my head. "Does this mean you really prefer to die?" I nodded. After a while, they stopped. Then I heard someone scream impatiently, "Okay, dress her up!"

The torture lasted for two hours, perhaps the longest two hours I ever experienced. While it was happening, I felt as though I was split into two — one part suffering, experiencing everything and yet refusing to give in, the other part detached, merely observing, planning out the next moves to be taken and answers to be given. It was as though my emotional passages were blocked. Only my mind was moving, rapidly, more rapid than usual.

After the whole painful process, elation dominated my spirit. I emerged the victor in the "political battle." I admitted nothing and divulged nothing. More importantly, I did not incriminate anyone. I felt as though I made up for all the past transgressions I committed in my life.

My emotions remained in check even days after the incident. I was not sure what was going to happen *next, whether someone was going to pick me up and torture me again. I conditioned and primed my emotions for any eventuality. My body, however, was exhibiting reactions. I couldn't stop myself from shaking whenever I narrate the incident. I always needed to take a deep breath to clear my chest. It took two whole weeks before I was finally able to cry. Before, tears were always about to fall, but would not.*

It was good that I felt elation after the torture, and not depression, weakening, extreme self-pity or guilt. I was able to sleep well. I was not bothered by nightmares. Perhaps it is because I regarded the whole experience as a "political battle" in which I won. Even then, I cannot discount the fact that my biggest morale booster was the tremendous support I received from my family and friends. My inherent sense of humor also made it easy for me to find something comical and ironic in such adverse situation.

It is saddening to know that there are victims of sexual molestation and rape who are treated by society with discrimination and censure. The victim is made to believe that her experience completely stained her personhood and lowered her physical and moral stature in society. She is even made to take the blame for what happened to her. People sometimes ask, "Wasn't there a way to prevent what happened," as though a blindfolded victim with her hands tied at the back and two attackers holding both her thighs can do anything!

We need to be vigilant in resisting any influence of our feudalistic culture which tend to look down on victims of sexual abuse. Perhaps we ourselves need to be more conscious that we do not send out derogatory messages to the victim as this will only aggravate an already pitiful situation. If a victim is not harboring such negative thoughts, these messages may implant themselves in her mind and serve to destroy her otherwise already balanced mental state. She may develop a low regard for herself because of such narrow-minded reactions which imply that her misfortune made her dirty and unworthy of anyone's respect. It is grossly unfair to blame the victim for a misfortune that she herself wished never happened.

A Prisoner's Song [1]

Ever since I entered this Manila City Jail,
My heart is always a well of sorrow.
Rise up in the morning, peer through the door,
My voice starts to quiver, the tears start to pour.

When the siren's call is heard,
We line up like cattle herd,
By fives a count is made, in case someone
    escaped.
What bitter sorrow it brings, to recall all these
    sufferings,
The pain of separation from the love of mother
    and siblings.

Amidst the long wait, Sunday comes,
Mother visits and to sorrow we both succumb,
Her face appears and to her I run,
In a tight embrace I hold her,
And my heart begins to weep and shudder.

---

[1] The lyrics of this song was written by a 51 year-old female detainee from Pampanga who was charged with complicity in a child kidnaping case. According to her, she was asked to take care of a child who later turned out to be a victim of a syndicate in the business of kidnapping and selling children. The arrest of the kidnapper led to the capture of this woman who was forced to admit to the crime after being subjected to water torture. *A Prisoner's Song* was recorded using the melody of an old song.

Many believe I truly am a kidnapper,
Though I am innocent, these words I cannot utter,
In jail I am and though someday I may be set
*   free,*
Friends and relations, for sure, will turn away
*   from me.*

But inside these prison walls, my mind has
*   blossomed,*
God's teachings I have planted in my mind and
*   in my bossom,*
And from an honest desire to understand my
*   Creator's word,*
Inside these prison walls his Voice I heard.

August 1989

Letters In and Out of Prison

MIRIAM RUTH M. DUGAY

July 31, 1987

Dear friends,

I write this message with contradictory emotions — sadness and happiness. Sad because I had to write this from prison at a time when the deep wounds inflicted on our lives by the past dictatorship are not yet healed, at the time the country got its first woman president who vowed never again to let the excesses of the past regime happen and to make human rights and social justice her government's utmost concerns.

Exactly a year ago today, the "new" Armed Forces of the Philippines' leading constabulary officers in Region 2 defied a court order for my release and went on to file trumped-up charges in court. It is so ironic that the military and the civilian authorities now say we have to go through the legal process to obtain my release when they were the first to defy and circumvent that same process.

Seventeen months after the people's uprising that saw the flight of an extremely unpopular dictator, human rights violations and mass poverty are still so much around and everywhere, and frighteningly worsening. The Government's economic and social policies essentially favor foreign investors and creditors and local big capitalists and landlords at the expense of workers, peasants and the rest of the least privileged Filipino people. These are the same policies that brought about and aggravated mass poverty among our people during the Marcos dictatorship.

Indeed, it is not only sad but painful as well that the these are happening under a government we put so much hope on, initially.

But experience teaches us to rely more on our united strength than wait for the mercy of the powers-that-be in realizing our rights. We derive strength and inspiration from each other's perseverance and determination in struggle, from each other's concern and reaching out, from each other's faith and hope in God's will. Someday we will overcome.

I am so happy and inspired because of the concern and support you are giving me, for sharing with me part of your thoughts and your time while I am in detention. I derive my strength and determination from our common faith and struggle.

Let our protest now be a protest not only against unjust detention but against all kinds of injustices committed against the least of God's people. Let us not settle for anything less than justice and dignity, as God intended for us no less.

In struggle and hope,

Miriam Ruth M. Angay

March 21, 1988

The Member Churches of the
National Council of Churches
in the Philippines

Dear brothers and sisters in Christ,

In reference to a resolution passed and approved by the
13th NCCP General Convention on November 25-27, 1987
urging the Government to hasten the process of justice for
me, and for my eventual release into the fold of my family
and into the Christian community, I would like to thank
you for such great concern and support.

The NCCP's efforts to alleviate my prison condition
and to work for my freedom were an indispensable factor in
the final resolution of my case in court last December 21,
1987. I was released on the same day.

But more than my physical freedom from prison is the
comfort and security I experienced, and continue to
experience, with the knowledge that I have not been alone
in my struggle.

It is comforting to know that the NCCP member
churches are ready to stand up and fight for justice where
it is due — on the side of the oppresed, and of those who
took the option for the oppressed.

Sincerely,

Miriam Ruth M. Angay

Ramblings of a Detainee

SHARON ROSE JOY RUIZ-DUREMDES

I closed my eyes as if to shut out the painful truth: a respectable Christian like me . . . locked behind bars! But the truth remained as surely as the iron bars I was clutching. In a span of twenty-four hours, I shed tears not a few times. But these were not tears of regret — no, I did not regret I was thrown in prison. For why should there be regrets when it was clear that I was there as a consequence of an act motivated by my religious convictions?

My comrades and I are released but we are not yet free — not by a long shot. (And so is everyone else in this country of ours.) Since that fateful day, many thoughts are racing through my mind: some questions but mostly realizations. Eleven of us were churchpeople. We were involved in a picket that led to our arrest. We were there because of our Christian beliefs. And we were taken in just like everyone else. We were subjected to the same inhuman treatment just like everyone else. We were condemned just like everyone else. It is very clear to me now that repression is totally encompassing. The state will spare no one, not even the church, in its attempt to silence those who work for change. Oh yes, they let a priest and a sister go — but isn't that all part of the scheme? To divide the church so they can rule?

I wondered why we were treated like common criminals even before we were tried. I thought a man was considered innocent before proven otherwise! Is it wrong to seek justice? Is it wrong to take back what rightfully belongs to you? Is it wrong to ask for a redress of grievances? In a free society, these are innate human rights and one need not ask permission to seek them even as one does not have to secure a permit to breathe the air around.

So, then, what can we say about a society that tramples upon God-given endowments enshrined as well in the law of the land? Would that society be cruel? Would it be unjust? Would you say it is unrighteous? Or maybe evil? Then, what does our divine mandate say we must do about an unrighteous system?

We went to the Jaro Police Station to talk as an educated adult would talk to another adult but we were met with insults, threats, blows, punches, fingernail scratches. What do these actions speak of? Fear? Panic? Defensiveness? I would like to think that this is an open admission on the part of the state of its increasing deterioration and the people's growing political consciousness. Pushed to the wall and threatened by the number of citizens who are finally seeing through the veneer of deception, the so-called defenders of the law violently unleashed their forces at us. Such is not a sign of strength. Rather, it is a sign of weakness. For if one is really strong . . . if one is really respected . . . if one is really loved, would there be need for force? It is so true that intensified repression is the state's main answer to the advancing struggle of our people.

In the evening of that never-to-be-forgotten day, most of the detainees laid their tired bodies to sleep if only to forget . . . temporarily. But sleep would not come to me. I thought of my two little children at home who would wake up in the middle of the night and not find their mother beside them — no one to cradle them and put them back to sleep. I thought of my husband nursing anger and bitterness and suppressing a natural response to fight back. I thought of my parents trying to make sense of the whole situation. As I lay there on the cold cement floor, I realized what it meant to take up my cross. Forsaking family and loved ones for the cause of God's people was for me a concrete fact . . . no longer a theological concept. But I knew that it was also because of them that I had to forsake them momentarily. The struggle was not primarily for me . . . I might not even be around to see the fruits of this struggle. But when the day of victory comes — when the state of affairs is transformed, then will my children experience a better life . . . then will they be able to claim the abundant life promised to them by God . . . then will I have contributed my little share in the work of renewal and change.

There were many beautiful off-shoots of our detention. We never lacked anything: food, beddings, moral boosters. But visible to me was the presence of people who, in times past, questioned my participation in the movement for change. Some waged smear campaigns against me and hurled back propaganda at me. Yes, on that day, they were right there — reaching out through the steel matting that separated us. At that very instance, there were tears of sympathy and concern . . . no accusing fingers, no "I told you so" remarks: evidences that they were beginning to see the legitimacy of action. As I squeezed their hands in gratitude, I was also asking: Must we wait until someone gets hurt before we get involved? Should there necessarily be a sacrificial lamb before we take action? And then John 12:24 came to me: " . . . unless a kernel of wheat falls to the ground and dies, it remains only a single seed. But if it dies, it produces many seeds. "

There were sixty people in that small uncomfortable enclosure and things could have been bad but there I saw a prototype of the social order we were all wanting to establish. A few hours after we were locked in, a "government" began to emerge. It was representative as all the sectoral leaders organized themselves into a Central Committee. Representing the churchpeople, I sat down with the leaders of the urban poor, the students, the peasants, the workers. Then we created "agencies" based on the real needs of the community: Food, Health, Security, Education. Again, each sector was represented in every committee. Every donation was centralized -- no one hoarded anything for himself or herself. Every donation was distributed equally

so no one would go hungry. Major decisions had to be made and all these were subjected to the group's consideration. There were many meetings. The Central Committee members were busy running back and forth from their constituents to the Central Committee bringing concerns of their sectors which were carefully discussed, analyzed and resolved.

Then word came that our only hope was to post bail at P200. 00 each. It was much higher than that. Thank God for the lawyers who pressured the fiscal to lower it. Could we all put up the money individually? The professionals said they could. The students, urban poor mothers, and peasants said it was impossible. Should the professionals go first and raise the amount for the others outside? The decision was to stick together — no one would leave unless everybody could. What a beautiful picture of solidarity! But within that solidarity was respect for every individual. One student got her release order early Tuesday morning, much to her surprise. Her mother went straight to the City Fiscal to submit her bail bond. As the student stepped out of the jail, there was no envy, no resentment, no bitterness . . . we were happy for her . . . we all knew she was a human being and was entitled to her rights.

As I walked out into the dingy cell into my husband's welcoming arms, mixed feelings gripped me. I was glad the nightmare was over but I knew I was merely walking into a much larger prison where my rights could be trampled upon again. There was no assurance of security out there. It was even safer inside the City Jail! But I knew I had grown an inch, nay, a foot, taller after being a victim. This was a victimization that only deepened my commitment to the cause of social transformation. This was an experience which only ignited a firm resolve to relentlessly work for the protection and promotion of people's rights. NO — there would be no turning back for me!

A Testimony on Hermon

CECILIA C. LAGMAN

Hermon Gaudencius Lagman was born on February 12, 1945. He was a consistent honor student from elementary to secondary school. He studied Political Science and pursued post-graduate studies in Law at the University of the Philippines. He passed the Bar in 1971.

During his student life, Hermon was active in various student activities. He took leadership of student organizations in campus and headed student papers including the Philippine Collegian and the Law Register of the University of the Philippines. His gift in writing was recognized in high school when he graduated as Poet of the Year.

As a law practitioner, Hermon represented labor unions such as those of La Tondeña and the Wack-Wack Country Club. He was among the original members of the Free Legal Assistance Group (FLAG) established by the late Jose W. Diokno. He was also member of church-related organizations as well as multi-sectoral groups like the Central Luzon Alliance for a Sovereign Philippines.

Hermon was apprehended and detained at Camp Crame, Camp General Aguinaldo, and finally at Camp Bonifacio from December 12, 1972 to February 12, 1973. He suspected that a man he knew back at UP during his student days precipitated his arrest and consequent detention. This man, who was then employed at Camp Aguinaldo, visited him a day before his abduction.

On the night of May 14, 1977, an anonymous telephone caller informed us that Hermon and his companion, Victor Reyes, were apprehended on their way to Pasay City to attend a meeting. The caller said he was with Hermon and Victor when they were being abducted but that he was able to escape from the military captors. This happened in the morning of May 11, 1977. Victor's mother saw her son (with whom Hermon was living at the time) and Hermon for the last time on that day at about 7:00 A.M. Their apartment was adjacent to the house of Victor's mother. Since then, nothing was heard of Hermon and Victor again.

I saw him last when I visited him on May 10, 1977.

We, Hermon's family, began the search on May 15, the day after the anonymous telephone call. We searched for him in all military camps, wrote letters of appeal to then President Marcos, Defense Secretary Enrile and AFP Chief of Staff General Ramos. We searched hard, but to no avail. All camp authorities denied having Hermon in their custody. But we knew they had him and maybe were still keeping him in some secret place or "safehouse."

We still hope to find our son Hermon, alive or dead — at least, his remains or bones.

It was more than 11 years ago when I received that telephone call. I remember how shocked and anguished I was by the realization that I might not see my son again. I still felt this way even though my family and I tried to prepare ourselves for this eventuality, knowing only too well of Hermon's unswerving militancy as an advocate for the working class.

At first I, along with other members of the family, was against him as a labor lawyer and as a human rights advocate. But he painstakingly explained his stand and showed this through examples he himself set. We saw in his deeds what he stood for and eventually understood him. And we became his faithful followers — staunch advocates of his principles.

I am certain that my son will be happy to know that his comrades in the ministry of the law for the protection of the oppressed and brutalized are resolute in perpetuating the gospel of truth, justice, freedom and democracy. He risked his life for this gospel. My son, however, never sought recognition. He only earnestly aspired for the fulfillment of his mission.

As I recall the short time my son was with us, I am inspired by two of his most important traits: his *commitment* to a valid and just cause, and his *fearlessness* in the pursuit and realization of his commitment.

Hermon's commitment to the cause of the working class was not of convenience but of conviction and compassion. He completely believed in his cause and in himself as an instrument to somehow further that cause. Hermon's commitment was of compassion because he had genuine love for the people he worked with and for. It was a matter of no small amusement within our family that for a lawyer and a bachelor, he was often short of money because he was so open-handed with his clients. He was always giving out lunch money, fare money, and others. He even paid for transcripts of stenographic notes and bail bonds for his invariably indigent clients.

I know that my son, although outwardly gentle and unassuming, was an angry young man. But his anger was not the mock of anger of a showman, but the strong, silent rage of a warrior.

Hermon was fearless in the pursuit and realization of his visions. I am not saying he was never afraid. I am sure he was, at one time or another, although he kept this from

us who were closest to him. What was important, I believe, is that he had the fortitude to do his duty, whatever evils beset or dangers lay before him.

At some dark hour, he faced the Ultimate Danger, nobly. We are proud of him.

I would like to think that all the *desaparecidos*[1], with Hermon as one of them, and all those who died for the same principle as his, are among this generation's imperishable children. They are the new sons and daughters of light — radiant with immortality. They are forever a part of the Filipino soul.

---

[1] *Desaparecidos* is a Spanish term for "the disappeared." The term was popularized in Latin America where cases of disappearances are rampant.

The Search for a Disappeared Son

IRENEA TAYAG

Our dream for our son, Carlos Tayag, was to be a priest. In his childhood days, I had to bring him to church to serve as an altar boy in the daily mass. After he finsihed his elementary grade as a Catholic school, I brought him to Manila to study for his priesthood at the abbey of Our Lady of Monserat at San Beda College. During his seven years in the abbey, everyhting was fine and things were going on smoothly.

After the Second Vatican Council convened by Pope John XXIII, I noticed some changes in him. This was the time of the Marcos regime when arbitrary killings, military atrocities, and other human rights violations were going on. Caloy, as our son was fondly called, was restless. He was looking for answers. He could no longer reconcile his monastic life with the social unrest in society.

When the situation worsened in 1970, he went on a regency. He increased his participation in rallies with some groups. He was involved in discussion groups between young Christians and students while studying at the University of the Philippines. My attitude towards him at the time ranged from confusion, disappointment, even anger. I was praying desperately, hoping against hope.

But when Caloy disappeared on August 17, 1976, I came to appreciate and understand more what he really stood and fought for.

His involvement in politics was not alien to his Christian beliefs. He did not risk his life merely for an ideology. He struggled for concrete goals. He lived a decent poverty, suffered hunger and experienced oppression.

All the pain and suffering I experienced in my search for my son brought in a new sense of purpose into my life: a firm determination to dedicate my life and family to a cause that will bring a light of hope to the lives of others. Now I am not after the physical Caloy, but the Caloy that is true and eternal. My search for Caloy, after all, was not in vain.

Vilma's Story

MARISSA PIRAMIDE

July 18, 1987. Under the noonday sun, Vilma and her husband Violeto were on their way, on foot, to the town of La Paz, Leyte. It is a four-to-five-hour walk from their place, Barangay Bocawon. They were going to buy a cavan of rice and some other foodstuffs. In a few days would be the baptism of their little girl and they must celebrate the day with some festive fare. They were almost halfway when they encountered a band of Alsa Masa. There must be about 50 in the group, Vilma figured. All of them were armed. The group was led by Raul whom Vilma and the rest of the folks knew to be a resident of La Paz. Patrolling bands of vigilantes are a common sight in the mountain barangays. Vilma thought this encounter now would just be uneventful, perhaps with the Alsa Masa asking a few questions. It was Raul who confronted the couple.

"Where are you going?"

"To town to buy rice and other needs."

"Remember, you were already warned repeatedly to buy just enough. Buying extra would mean you're providing food to the NPA (New People's Army). And how many times were you advised to transfer residence to the town center? You mountainfolks are so hard-headed!"

"We'd move to the town if we have a place to stay there and if we're assured of our livelihood."

"You don't have to worry about that; we'll help you... Now, (addressing Violeto) you must come with us. We're going to take you to the *municipio*. Don't you worry (addressing Vilma), your husband will be back in three days."

Bocawon is a remote mountain *barangay* of La Paz. Residing there are some 40 households, mostly peasants. The couple Vilma and Violeto till a three-hectare land owned by the latter's grandfather. They plant rice, corn and some root crops. They also raise vegetables and chickens. When not working in their farm, Vilma and Violeto would be joining in the *alayon* at someone else's field. A day's work of one person would usually be exchanged with one chicken. Thus, the couple was able to acquire a sizable flock of chickens. Almost every Thursday, which is market day in La Paz, Vilma would go to town to sell vegetables and other produce. She would go back home with the family's needs for the week. Vilma and Violeto have two kids, a four-year old boy and a two-year old girl.

Then the Alsa Masa came. Counter-insurgency operations used to be conducted by the military alone. Now there is the Alsa Masa. Oftentimes, the military and Alsa Masa together would conduct joint operations. The Alsa Masa operations went on for two months (May to June 1987) in neighboring *barangays*. They raided houses of peasants and took away household articles and valuables. Strafing houses was common, both day and nighttime. Some of the menfolk were salvaged. But the Alsa Masa were not yet in Bocawon, apparently because the place is too far up in the mountains. But in June 1987, the *barangay* captain of Bocawon was killed. Real fear crept into Bocawon.

It was around 4:00 P.M. when the Alsa Masa, with Violeto, reached the *municipio* of La Paz. Vilma also went with the group. Violeto was entrusted to the police. Both husband and wife had no idea what was to happen next. Violeto advised his wife to go back home that evening and come back the next day. In case he would be detained, Violeto bade Vilma to bring him food and clothes. And yes, Vilma should take the children with her when she comes back. Vilma then set out for the long walk back to Bocawon. It was late when she reached home, about 11:00 P.M.

The next day Vilma brought her children to their grandparents who were residing in another *barangay*. Then she proceeded to the town. It was about 11:00 A.M. when she reached the *municipio*. She was told by the guard that her husband was released the night before. She managed to make a hasty inquiry from the other detainees. She learned that the Alsa Masa came back that night and forcibly took Violeto away; and that Violeto did not want to come out. He clung to the posts, the bars, and the door, but he was taken anyhow.

Vilma wasted no time. She searched for her husband among relatives in the town. Failing to find him, she went to the other towns. She even reached Tacloban City, surmising that Violeto might seek refuge with relatives there. It took Vilma four days of lonely, fruitless search. Her pocket money, P300, was almost gone now. The amount left was just enough to bring her back to La Paz. She decided to return to La Paz.

Reaching the town she was met with a piece of news: there are two dead bodies near (or was it under?) a tree by the road that leads to Barangay Camparik. The place is about one kilometer away. This time Vilma's parents came to accompany her. They trekked the dirt road towards Camparik until they came upon the said tree. Hanging from a branch was a body, headless. Right away Vilma knew it was Violeto. She recognized the shirt. At the foot of the tree was the head, fragmented. The skull was chopped into five parts, presumably by a sharp-bladed *bolo*. One other dead body was lying nearby.

Vilma could not recall at all how she felt and reacted to the gruesome sight. The most immediate concern was to bury Violeto. They brought Violeto's remains to the *municipio*. The chief of police simply advised them to go straight to the cemetery. He said there was no more need to go through the formalities in the *municipio* since the body was already decomposing and stinking. Wrapped in a *banig* and carted on a carabao, Violeto's remains were brought to the cemetery and interred unceremoniously. That was July 24, six days after Violeto was taken by the Alsa Masa.

After the burial, Vilma came to stay with her parents. There they started the traditional nightly prayers for the dead which was joined in by neighbors and relatives. At these nightly gatherings some Alsa Masa would accost Vilma with threats that she too would soon be arrested for being an NPA; but should she join Alsa Masa, nothing would happen to her. She was told that she would receive some money and that her children would be assured of their daily food.

Vilma did not wait for long, she decided to leave the place. On July 28, even before the prayers for her late husband were completed, she and the children, accompanied by her father, left for Tacloban. There they took the boat bound for Manila.

Back in Bocawon, Vilma thinks back, life was just all right and things went well with them. There they tilled the land. They knew what to plant and raise in the farm. And they harvested what they planted. With more industry and hard work, Vilma and Violeto believed they could very well provide for their growing family. As mother, wife and peasant, Vilma believed Bocawon was where she belonged. She was there at

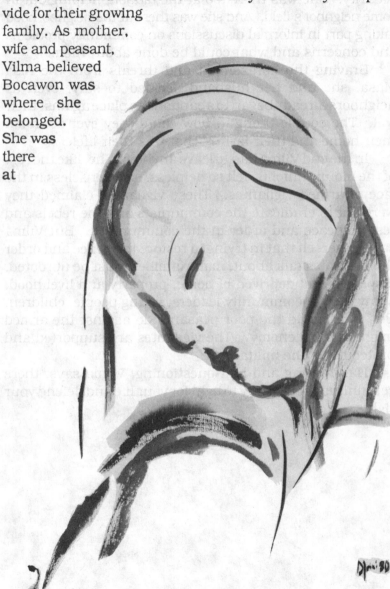

the farm with her husband, making the land productive with their toil and their aspiration to attain decent living. She was there at home with her husband and children, building a family life founded on care, love, support and security. She was there too at the *alayon*, helping out in some neighbor's field. And she was there at the neighborhood taking part in informal discussions on community problems and concerns and what could be done about them.

Braving the harassment and threats from the Alsa Masa, she and her husband decided to stay, even as neighbors already began to abandon the place against their will. The couple thought, how could they ever abandon their home and their farm? That was their life!

In the end Vilma had to leave anyhow. She, like the rest of the mountainfolks, felt so helpless, so defenseless in the face of armed vigilantes. These vigilantes claimed they were out to eradicate the communists and the rebels and restore peace and order in the communities. But Vilma saw for herself that in trying to restore the peace and order the vigilantes talk about, many families must be uprooted, displaced and deprived of home, property and livelihood. Many died — community leaders, young people, children. But what could the poor peasants do against the armed might of their enemy? The vigilantes are supported and protected by the military.

Half-hinting and half-questioning, Vilma says, there certainly must be a way to fight for your life and defend your rights.

"Wala Na Bang Katapusan Ang Aming Paghihintay?"

*L*imang matatapang na babae, pawang mga kasapi ng
FIND, o **Families of Victims of Involuntary Disappearances**, ang dito'y nagbahagi ng kanilang mga karanasan at
pananaw tungkol sa pagkawala ng kanilang mga asawa.
May kinalamang pulitikal ang mga karanasang ito sapagkat
aktibo sa iba't ibang pakikibakang pulitikal ng mamamayan
ang kanilang mga asawa.

Sina Erlinda, Corazon, Milagros, Emily at Lorena ay ilan
lamang sa dumaraming bilang ng mga kaanak na hanggang
ngayon ay umaasa pa ring matatagpuan ang kanilang mga
mahal sa buhay. Ngunit sa kabila ng kahirapang dulot ng
ganitong karanasan, makikitang sila ngayo'y aktibo na ring
kalahok sa pagtataguyod ng karapatang tao.

Erlinda Yandoc

Ang aking asawang si Reynaldo ay dating nag-oorganisa sa hanay ng mga propesyonal. Kinuha siya ng mga sundalo sa Barangay Lawa, Obando, Bulacan noong ika-20 ng Mayo, 1984. Ilang oras bago nangyari ito, dinampot ng mga sundalo ang kanyang mga kasamang sina Danilo Deldoc, ang pasyenteng si Jose de la Cruz at asawang Perlita paglabas nila ng Manila Medical Center sa Taft Avenue. Pagkaraan ng ilang oras, nalaman ko mula sa aking mga anak na kinuha ang kanilang tatay sa aming bahay. Napag-alaman namin na ang dumampot sa kanila ay mga sundalo ng Presidential Security Command. Kung saan-saan kami naghanap subalit walang nangyari.

Makalipas ang ilang linggo, nabalitaan naming may in-*ambush* na tatlong tao sa Cabatuan City, Palayan. Napag-alaman naming ang mga ito ay sina Danny at ang mag-asawang de la Cruz. Ngunit nang pinuntahan ng asawa ni Danny ang bangkay, sinabi ng mga taga-punerarya na kinuha na ito ng mga sundalo ng Philippine Constabulary. Mula noon ay wala na kaming nabalitaan tungkol kay Danny. Subalit nalaman naming may sinunog na bangkay noong panahon ding iyon. Ang mga katawan naman ng mag-asawang de la Cruz ay kinuha ng kanilang kamag-anak.

Limang taon na ang nakakaraan. Hanggang sa kasalukuyan ay wala pa rin akong balita sa aking asawa. Alam kong wala siyang ginawang masama laban sa kanyang kapwa. Ang tangging alam ko ay tumutulong siya sa mga naaapi. Hindi namin alam kung siya ay buhay pa o patay na. Masakit, mahirap ang mawalan ng *padre de familia*. Mayroon kaming tatlong anak. Lagi nilang tinatanong kung buhay pa ang kanilang tatay. Kailan kaya magkakaroon ng katarungan ang pagkawala ng aming mahal sa buhay?

Corazon Estojero

Nawala ang aking asawang si Edgardo noong ika-14 ng Nobyembre, 1987. Isa siyang organisador ng KMU (Kilusang Mayo Uno) sa Parañaque Labor Alliance. Bago naganap ang mga pangyayari, sinabi ng aming kapitbahay na may isang linggo nang may nakaistambay na mga lalaking malalaki ang katawan sa kanto malapit sa aming bahay. Nang panahong iyon ay hindi na siya madalas umuwi sa amin dahil alam niyang tinatarget na siya ng militar. Alam din niyang may kapitbahay kaming *vigilante*.

Malaki ang naging epekto ng kanyang pagkawala. Tatlo ang aming anak. Dalawa at kalahating taong gulang pa lamang ang aming bunso at umiinom pa ng gatas. Nag-iisa na lang akong naghahanapbuhay ngayon. Hindi ito sumasapat para sa pang-upa ng bahay, gastos sa pagkain at panggatas ng bata. Ang panganay kong anak na labing tatlong taong gulang ay nasa ikalawang antas ng *high school*. Napakahirap ang mag-isa sa paghahanap-buhay, lalung-lalo na ngayong patuloy ang pagtaas ng presyo ng mga bilihin.

Naniniwala akong ang problema ng aking pamilya ay nakakabit sa problemang panlipunan at ng mamamayang Pilipino. Marami ang nadudukot, nasa-salvage, nasusupil sa iba't-ibang paraan para mapigil lamang ang paghahanap ng katotohanan. Kung sino ang gumagawa ng mabuti, siya ang masama, at ang gumagawa ng kasamaan ang siyang nananaig.

Naniniwala akong darating ang panahong maiaahon ko ang aking pamilya mula sa kahirapan tungo sa maaliwalas na bukas. Isang kinabukasang may tunay na kalayaan at demokrasya.

MILAGROS RELOJ

Ang walang katarungang pagkakadukot sa aking asawang si Enrique noong ika-7 ng Abril, 1988 ay isang pangyayaring hindi ko malilimutan habang ako'y nabubuhay. Naganap ang pangyayari sa pagitan ng 4:00 at 5:00 ng hapon sa *basketball court* katapat mismo ng aming tahanan sa Dagat-dagatan, Malabon. Kasalukuyan siyang nanonood ng basketball nang bigla na lamang lapitan siya ng apat na mga lalaking nakasibilyan at armado ng kalibre .45 at *armalite*. Walang tanung-tanong at tinutukan na lamang siyang bigla, habang may isang kotseng kulay *maroon* na humintong bigla sa tapat nila. Sapilitan nilang isinakay si Rick na patuloy na nagpupumiglas. Nagtakbuhan sa pag-kabigla ang mga taong nanonood at naglalaro. Sila man ay inambaan ng *armalite*.

Isinigaw nilang nahuli si Rick. Nakarating ito sa aking pandinig, at dali-dali akong tumakbo patungo sa *basketball court*. Hindi ko na naisip na may sanggol akong dinadala sa aking sinapupunan na noon ay anim na buwan na. Hindi ko na inatubili ang aking kalagayan dahil nais kong tulungan agad ang aking asawa. Ngunit hindi ko na naga-wang makalapit sa kanya dahil pinigilan ako ng aming mga kapit-bahay. Natakot sila nang itinuon sa akin ng mga lalaking armado ang kanilang baril. Inilayo na lang ako ng aming mga kapitbahay. Wala na akong nagawa kundi ang magsisigaw. Naisip kong nailagay ko sa panganib ang sanggol sa aking sinapupunan sa pangyayaring iyon. Hindi ko maubos-maisip kung ano ang mangyayari sa akin kung sa pagkawala ng aking asawa ay mawawala rin ang aking anak.

Malaki ang naging epekto ng pangyayaring ito sa aming komunidad. Si Rick ay kabilang sa isang organi-sasyong naglalayong ilayo ang mga kabataan mula sa mga masasamang bisyo tulad ng paggamit ng bawal na gamot, sugal, alak, at iba pa. Bilang isang organisador, unti-unting nahikayat ni Rick ang mga kabataan sa mga gawaing may kabuluhan tulad ng mga larong pampalakasan. Nakatulong din siyang imulat sila sa kahalagahan at mga tungkulin ng isang kabataan sa ating bansa. Ngunit muling nagkawatak-watak at nawalan ng sigla ang mga kabataan mula nang madukot si Rick. Para sa kanila, isang tunay na lider ang nawala sa aming lugar. Nagkaroon na rin sila ng takot at pangamba na baka mangyari din sa kanila ang nangyari kay Rick, lalo na't kapag may sasakyang tumitigil sa aming lugar. Ang dating saya at sigla sa aming komunidad ay biglang nawala.

Nais ko ipaabot sa mga pamilya na naging biktima ng ganitong pangyayari na tayo ay di dapat mawalan ng pag-asa. Sa awa't tulong ng Poong Maykapal at sa sama-sama nating pagkilos ay matatagpuan natin ang ating mga mahal sa buhay. Makakamit din natin ang tunay na hustisya para sa ikatatahimik hindi lamang ng ating kalooban, kundi pati na rin ng ating bansa.

EMILY GARCIA

Ang aking asawang si Reynaldo ay dalawampu't apat na taong gulang nang siya ay mawala. Dinukot siya noong ika-28 ng Marso, siyam na buwan pagkaraan ng aming kasal. Walong buwan na noon ang bata sa aking sina-pupunan. Nawala si Reggie nang panahong may kampanya ang pamahalaang Aquino laban sa paglaganap ng mga *Sparrow Units.* Ayon sa pamahalaan, ang mga *Sparrow* daw ay nakabase sa mga mahihirap na komunidad dito sa Kamaynilaan.

Ayon sa mga saksi, si Reggie ay hinarang ng mga lalaking may matitipunong pangangatawan, disenteng manamit at naka-gupit militar habang naglalakad siya sa kanto ng N. Domingo at F. Manalo sa San Juan. Pinilit siyang isakay sa isa sa mga kotseng diumano'y naghihintay na roon mula pa ika-5:00 ng umaga. Nagtangkang lumaban si Reggie ngunit sinuntok siya sa kanyang sikmura sa pamamagitan ng isang baril. Isang lalaki naman ang mabilis na ipinukpok ang kanyang baril sa batok ni Reggie. Nawalan siya ng malay. Naisakay nila sa kotse si Reggie. Ayon din sa mga nakakita, nagtungo sa direksyon ng Aurora Boulevard ang mga kotse.

Lumapit kami sa mga awtoridad upang ipagbigay-alam ang pangyayari at humingi ng tulong. Nagpunta kami sa San Juan Police Station, Camp Crame, Camp Bagong Diwa sa Bicutan, at iba pang kampo ng militar. Lumapit rin kami sa National Bureau of Investigations (NBI) ngunit wala kaming natamong positibong tugon mula sa kanila. Sa halip ay nabastos pa kami sa aming ginagawang paghahanap at pagtatanong. Naghanap din kami sa mga morge ngunit wala pa ring magandang resulta. Nag-sampa na rin kami ng kaso sa Presidential Commission on Human Rights (PCHR) at hanggang ngayon ay naghihintay pa rin kami ng kanilang aksyon o imbestigasyon.

Si Reggie ay isang *community organizer*. Aktibo siyang kumilos sa hanay ng mga istudyante-kabataan. Kumilos din sa hanay ng mga maralitang taga-lunsod. Matagal siyang kumilos para sa mga mahihirap. Maraming siyang paghihirap na dinanas sa pag-oorganisa, tulad ng pagkaka-kulong ng may dalawang linggo at pagkakasakit bunga ng *torture*. Naaalala ko pa na madalas siyang mangarap ng magandang bukas para sa aming mga anak. Nakita niyang matutupad ang kanyang pangarap sa pamamagitan ng paglalaan ng kanyang buong panahon at maging buhay tungo sa isang maayos at masaganang lipunan. Iyon na raw ang kanyang maipamamana sa magiging anak ng aming mga anak.

Mahigit nang isang taon ngayon si Remelyn. Hindi man lamang nakita ni Reggie ang aming anak. Madalas tanungin sa akin ni Remelyn kung nasaan ang kanyang ama. Paano ko sasagutin ang tanong ng isang batang wala pang nauunawaan sa mga nagaganap sa kanyang paligid? Sasabihin ko bang ang kanyang ama ay patay na o buhay pa kung ako mismo ay hindi nakatitiyak?

Alam kong dumanas din o dumaranas pa ng *torture* ang aking asawa at ang iba pang biktimang tulad niya. Kaming mga pamilya na kanilang iniwan ay dumaranas naman ng *mental torture*. Ibayong hirap ng loob ang aming nadarama — pagdadalamhati, tensiyon, awa sa mga anak at sa sarili, galit, paghihiganti. Dagdag pa rito ang problema ng dislokasyon sa pinansiya.

Hindi pa rin matiwasay ang aming isipan. Kung sila man ay patay na, marahil ay magkakaroon kami ng kaunting kapanatagan kung sila ay aming makikita at maililibing nang marangal. Ngunit higit kaming mapapanatag kung mabibigyan ng katarungan ang aming mga asawa at iba pang biktima ng ganitong karahasan. Magkakaroon ng ganitong katarungan kung maparurusahan ang mga taong may kinalaman at direktang may kagagawan sa kanilang puwersadong pagkawala!

LORENA LOPEZ

Nawala si Jaime noong ika-20 ng Marso, 1987. May 35 taong gulang siya noon. Dati siyang nagtuturo ng katekismo. Isa rin siyang *community organizer* at kalahok sa kampanya ni Lean Alejandro ng Partido ng Bayan. Mayroon kaming tatlong supling — si Redentor, 5 taon; si Patnubay Liwanag, 3 taon; at si Jaime Jr., 2 taon.

Si Jaime ay isang responsableng asawa't ama. Isinabubuhay niya ang kanyang mga prinsipyo at sinisikap na maigpawan ang pagiging makasarili at iba pang kahinaan. Si Jaime ay larawan ng isang gurong nagsasabuhay ng kanyang itinuturo. Siya ay kalahok sa pag-oorganisa at pagmumulat ng malawak na masa. Tuwiran siyang nakalubog sa hanay ng mga maralita para sa pagbabago sa lipunan. Mayroon siyang matatag na paninindigan laban sa lahat ng uri ng pagsasamantala.

Malapit ko nang isilang ang aming bunsong anak nang mawala si Jaime. Lumipas muna ang tatlong araw bago

namin nalaman na siya ay nawawala. Wala kaming sina-
yang na sandali sa paghahanap nang malaman namin ang
nangyari sa kanya. Nagtungo kami sa mga kampo ng
militar, mga istasyon ng pulisya, mga bilangguan, mga
ospital, at pati na sa mga morge. Nag-sampa na rin kami
ng kaso sa Presidential Commission on Human Rights.
Dumulog na rin kami sa Pangulong Cory Aquino. Pawang
mga kabiguan ang aming natamo sa aming paghahanap.
Nawalan na kami ng tiwala sa pamahalaan at maging sa
iba pang ahensiya ng gobyerno. Mabuti na lamang at may
mga kaibigan at kamag-anak na tumutulong sa amin.
Nariyan din ang iba't ibang *human rights organizations*
tulad ng FIND.

Liban sa pangungulila, malaki rin ang naging dislokasyon sa aming pangkabuhayan. Si Jaime, bagama't
kumikilos, ay naghahanapbuhay din para sa amin. Sa
akin ngayon nakabalikat ang lahat ng responsibilidad ng
pagpapamilya. Nagtitinda ako ngayon ng mga damit,
processed meat, at iba pang maaaring pagkakitaan.

Para akong naputulan ng pakpak nang mawala ang
aking asawa. Paano na kaya kaming mag-iina ngayon?
Madalas magtanong ang mga bata kung kailan uuwi ang
kanilang ama. Paano ko sasabihin na walang katiyakan
ang pag-uwi ng kanilang tatay? Hindi lamang ang mga
bata ang nagtatanong nang ganito. Ako rin ay nagtatanong
kung siya ay babalik pa. Nasaan na kaya siya ngayon?
Pinahihirapan kaya siya ng mga dumukot sa kanya?

Tinatanaw ko na ang lahat ng ito ay matatapos rin.
May mga maniningil sa mga berdugong naging sanhi ng
pagkawala ng aking asawa. Darating ang panahong iyan,
alam ko.

Ang kaso ng aking asawa ay isa lamang sa dumaraming
kaso ng paglabag sa makataong karapatan ng mamamayang
Pilipino, lalo na ng mga manggagawa at anakpawis. Ang
pagkawala ni Jaime ay malinaw na pagpapatunay ng
kapabayaan, pagsasamantala at pagsasawalang-kibo ng
pamahalaan at mga ahente nito sa mga umaalingawngaw

na isyu ng karapatang tao. Hindi man sabihin, direktang may pananagutan ang pamahalaan sa nangyari sa aking asawa at sa iba pang biktima ng pwersadong pagkawala. Nasaan ang sinasabing pagbabago at demokrasya sa ilalim ng bagong rehimen? Bakit sa panahon pa ng isang "demokratikong" pamahalaan nawala ang aking asawa?

EDITORS' TRANSLATION:

"Will Our Search Ever End?"

Five courageous women, all members of FIND, or **Families of Victims of Involuntary Disappearances**, *here have given testimonies on their experiences and views on the forced disappearance of their husbands. These experiences are political in nature because their husbands were all active in various political struggles of the people.*

Erlinda, Corazon, Milagros, Emily and Lorena are only a few among the growing number of relatives of victims of forced disappearances who are still hoping that they would someday find their loved ones. But inspite of the hardships that these experiences have brought onto their lives, these women have come to be active participants in the promotion of human rights — the cause for which their husbands made extreme sacrifice.

ERLINDA YANDOC

We live in Barangay Lawa, Obando, Bulacan. My husband, Reynaldo, was picked up by soldiers of the Presidential Security Command from our house on May 20, 1984. This occurred a few hours after three of his companions were similarly abducted as they were living the Manila Medical Center. I learned a few weeks later that Rey's three companions were ambushed and killed by the military.

My family and I searched everywhere for Rey. But we found nothing. After five years, I still have no information on the whereabouts of my husband. Our three children would always ask me if their father is still alive. I know that Rey did not do anything wrong except to work with the oppressed in our community. He was an organizer among the ranks of professionals.

Still waiting, I ask: will there be justice in the loss of our loved one?

CORAZON ESTOJERO

I learned that my husband, Edgardo, was missing on November 14, 1987. For weeks before this happened, our house was being watched by suspicious-looking men. Edgardo tried to stay inside the house as much as possible because he already knew that he was a target of the military. He also knew that there was a vigilante in our neighborhood.

Edgardo and I have three children, the youngest of whom is only two and a half years old. It is difficult to be the lone breadwinner in the family, especially now that prices of commodities continue to rise.

These difficulties did not hinder me from facing problems. I believe that problems in family are related to the problems in society. Nowadays, it is common to witness indiscriminate killings and violations of human rights just to suppress the search for truth. I believe there will come a better tomorrow for my family. A brighter future where there is true freedom and democracy.

MILAGROS RELOJ

The blatant abduction of my husband, Enrique, on April 7, 1988 was an incident I will never forget for as long as I live.

Rick was at the time watching a game at the neighborhood basketball court. Suddenly, four armed plainclothesmen approached and pointed guns at him. They forced him to get inside a waiting car. The other people scampered in fear to safer places as they were also threatened with guns.

I was doing housechores then when I heard the commotion from the basketball court. When I learned that Rick was being taken away, I ran towards them. At that time it did not occur to me that I was six-months pregnant. All that mattered to me then was to be with Rick and help him. But our neighbors held me back when they saw the armed men pointing their guns at me. All I could do was look as they took my husband away. There was nothing I could do but cry and scream in desperation. I later realized that I endangered the baby in my womb during that incident. I cannot imagine how I would have coped with the pain of losing Rick and my baby at the same time.

Rick's disappearance had a big effect in our community. As a youth organizer, he was able to lure our young people away from anti-social activities like drug abuse, gambling, theft, and alcohol to more socially productive involvements. When Rick disappeared, our youth lost the inspiration they found in him as a leader. Moreover, they were overcome by constant fear that the same thing might also happen to them.

I would like to speak to those families with the same experience. We should not lose hope. With God's help and mercy and our collective action, we will soon find our disappeared loved ones. We will achieve genuine justice, not only for our inner peace, but also for the peace of our nation.

EMILY GARCIA

My husband Reynaldo was 24 years old when he disappeared. He was abducted on March 28, 1987, nine months after we got married. I was then eight months pregnant with our first child.

Reggie disappeared during the Government's campaign against Sparrow Units which were believed to be based in poor communities in Metro Manila. According to witnesses, Reggie was abducted by armed men while he was walking along the corner of N. Domingo and F. Manalo streets in San Juan.

We approached authorities to inform them of the incident and to seek assistance. We went to the San Juan Police Station, Camps Crame and Bagong Diwa, and other military camps. We also went to the National Bureau of Investigations. We searched the morgues. We filed a case at the Presidential Commission on Human Rights (PCHR). All our efforts bore no positive results. Instead, our appeals were met with indifference and ridicule. Up to now, we are still waiting for PCHR's investigation on the case.

Reggie was a community organizer. His work with students and the urban poor led to his arrest and detention. He became seriously ill as a result of torture. I still remember how he used to dream of a brighter future for the children we will have. He knew that he would realize his dreams by offering his full time and even his life. He said this will be the legacy he will leave behind for the children of his children.

Our only child, Remelyn, is now more than two years old. Reggie never saw her. She would always ask me where her father is. How can I answer the questions of a child who still does not understand what is happening around her? Should I say that her father is still alive when I myself am not sure if he is?

I know that my husband and other victims like him experienced or are still experiencing torture. We, the families they left behind, on the other hand, are suffering from mental torture. Everyday we find ourselves going through feelings of grief, tension, anger, revenge, self-pity, pity for our children. Then there is also the problem of financial dislocation.

Our minds are still restless. If our loved ones are already dead, perhaps we will have some peace of mind if we can find their bodies and give them a decent burial. But if justice will be served those guilty of these crimes, then perhaps we can experience a more lasting peace.

LORENA LOPEZ

Jaime disappeared on March 20, 1987. He was 35 years old then. He used to teach catechism. He was also a community organizer, and was active in the campaign program of Lean Alejandro of the *Partido ng Bayan* (People's Party) during the Congressional elections in 1987. We have three children — Redentor, aged five; Patnubay Liwanag, aged three; and Jaime Jr., two.

Jaime was a responsible father and husband. He lived out his principles and tries to overcome selfishness and other weaknesses. He was a model teacher who taught by example. He was involved in the organizing and education of the masses, and was directly immersed in the lives of the poor. He held a strong conviction against any form of exploitation.

I was about to give birth to our youngest child when I learned he was missing. We did not waste time to look for him after we received information about his disappearance. We searched in military camps, hospitals and morgues. We filed a case at the Presidential Commission on Human Rights, and even appealed to President Aquino. All our efforts were futile. We lost trust in the Government. But we are fortunate that there are friends, relatives and human rights organizations like FIND who continue to help and support us.

It seemed like my wings were clipped when Jaime disappeared. I often wondered how long my children and I will survive. They always ask me when their father would come home. How can I tell them that there is no certainty in their father's return? I also constantly wonder if Jaime is still alive.

I look ahead and I see that our sufferings will one day end. There will come a time when the perpetrators of my husband's disappearance will pay for their crimes. That time will come. I know.

The case of my husband is just one of the many cases of human rights violations. Jaime's disappearance is a clear manifestation of the Government's negligence and indifference towards issues of human rights. Even if Government continues to deny it, they have direct responsibility over what happened to Jaime. Where are the changes and the democracy we so proudly claim to be enjoying under President Corazon Aquino? Why did my husband disappear during the incumbency of a supposed democratic government?

Women and
their Struggle for
Human Rights

In Search of Authentic Discipleship

Victoria Narciso-Apuan

Last night I was crying in my sleep. It was a night full of anguish. I could not forget the disturbing news that two women arrested by the military on suspicion that they were Communists were raped and tortured to make them "confess" to their alleged crimes against the state. The news had a greater impact on me because I personally know one of them. According to those who visited her, her head was banged several times against a wall so that she would periodically doze off while talking to her visitors. The other woman now has trouble urinating because of the continual molestation of her sexual organs. "Spare them from further harm, O Lord," I prayed. "Punish those animals who continue to maltreat them!"

I look back on my own awakening to the issue of human rights. It started when I began to subscribe to the *Malaya* newspaper a couple of years ago — Marcos' time. The newspaper had a Human Rights Monitor then. I had one sleepless night after reading about a woman whose breasts were found sliced off by the military. Why? Because she was considered a subversive. Again and again I read the reports, and everytime I shuddered at the thought that there were Filipinos who, in reality, were beasts rather than persons. Yet they continue to go unpunished. I asked myself then, "Will this ever end? Will justice ever reign in our land?"

I get easily touched by the underdogs of society. Perhaps this is a product of my Christian upbringing. I would watch television and find myself crying when a character in the program is terribly oppressed just because that person did not have the right family name nor large amounts of cash or assets. My friends used to say that it is not always good to have a "soft heart" as the world is sometimes brutal to those who are compassionate. Recalling those warnings, I realize that in my youth I lacked the necessary complement of compassion — a highly critical mind. One is called not only to love and serve the poor but to know why they are poor in the first place and, more importantly, to work for a society where poor people no longer exist.

An egalitarian society? Oooh . . . that was (and continues to be) considered a radical concept. Yet I look at the man from Nazareth and realize that indeed, he was radical. Who was he? A Holy Saturday editorial in one newspaper described Christ's story:

> "The story of Christ is essentially the simple story of a man who tried to espouse ideas contrary to the established belief, and as a consequence, was hunted by the authorities. Until he was caught, he had no fixed residence, he had to stay most of the time with people and crowds to escape arrest. When the authorities finally caught up with him, they mocked and humiliated him, first in order to destroy his credibility and later, crucified him.... But he died proclaiming his belief." *(Manila Chronicle 18/04/87)*

The editorial went on to lament that our present Christian tradition "has deviated, and has even vulgarized, Christianity. For many years, the political dimension of Christ's martyrdom — the fight with the Pharisees, the scheming intrigues of those in power who colluded with the propertied elite — was ignored."

I continue to read stories about our present-day martyrs — people who were discredited, harassed and killed because they dared to follow the example of Jesus of Nazareth; because they dared to dream of the Kingdom; and because they dared to espouse and promote ideas contrary to established beliefs. If the articles focus on women, I cut out the stories and file them, just as I do not want to forget the suffering of these authentic disciples.

Going into human rights work is a messy endeavor. Now, more than before, it is quite unpopular because it uncovers the unpleasant aspects of our society which continues today even after the departure of Marcos: that of the unequal distribution of God's creation and the world's goods, the corruption *Authentic discipleship today means to choose to be as radical as Jesus* inherent in government bureaucracy, and the increasing assaults of foreign intervention. Human rights work challenges people to open their eyes and view the mutilated bodies of victims of armed fanatical groups and vigilantes, to be at the wake of the massacre victims of Mendiola, to interview the men, women and children who lost their homes, carabaos, loved ones and limbs because of bombings and strafings in their communities. And in all these to weep, to feel nauseated, and at times to be so angry as to utter a bad word for the perpetrators of the crimes.

It is messy, because a person engaged in human rights advocacy is always a potential victim of human rights violations. Many human rights workers and advocates themselves become statistics in the Human Rights Monitor.

I belong to the Christians for the Realization of a Sovereign Society or CROSS. It was engaged one time in a fact-finding mission on the victims of secret marshals (policemen in plain clothes) in the summer of 1985. We documented over 30 cases. A report on this was subsequently published in a Sunday magazine. The Catholic Bishops Conference of the Philippines made a public statement denouncing these secret marshals and asserted the human being's right to life. By October of that year, the military accused CROSS of being subversive.

It took several months to get over my initial fear. Never in my wildest dreams did I ever expect to be branded a subversive. I wanted to hide and lie low . . . but I realized that this was precisely what the military wanted — to quell the growing human rights movement. By sowing fear and discrediting genuine nationalist movements, it seeks to eventually paralyze people. I shared this feeling with others, and we also shared each other's strength. Soon, I overcame my fear. I remembered Jesus who, on his way to Jerusalem, "grit his teeth" and pledged to continue.

I am more at home with fear now. It still comes, but I am no longer paranoid. I am still with CROSS. Now I plan to tap and organize more middle-class Christians like myself for programs and projects which aim to build peace that is based on justice. It is a special mission to help these privileged people — who have stable jobs and eat three to five times a day and have firm roofs over their heads — to realize that the call to discipleship as defined by Jesus to the rich young man is still as valid today as it was two thousand years ago. Jesus asked, and continues to ask, for total commitment and detachment. Jesus bids us to re-examine our life choices, lifestyles and relationships according to God's standard: the common good.

Peace is a wonderful idea to imagine. However, it is justice which is concretely felt, experienced and measured.

Justice means more food on the table, security of life and health, economic and political democracy. Justice means ensuring one's right to a dignified and humane living condition. Therefore, peace with justice means no more human rights violations! It means **shalom** in its original and all-encompassing term — **shalom** promoted not just in people's hearts and minds but also in social, economic and political structures.

People who know me well attribute the song "Sangandaan" (Crossroad) as my personal anthem. "Sangandaan" begins by recalling the period in one's life when life was simple, when one sought eternal life only. Then one's desire to love more deeply leads one to a crossroad. A choice has to be made: to live one's life with only personal salvation, or to work for the liberation of humankind. Every crossroad is a crisis of faith and lifestyle because only one road must be taken. This decision can either lead to happiness or frustration. To choose social transformation is to choose a more complicated lifestyle.

Yes, my life is a series of crossroads. With these cross-roads arise major and minor crises, major and minor decisions. I realize that as I work for the promotion and defense of the rights of others, I also need to come to terms with my own rights as woman, whether at home, at work, or in the Church. I find myself asserting my personal rights as well! What sustains me in my personal and communal journey is the thought that I have but one life to live and I must live it as intensely and as single-mindedly as Jesus did.

During the time of the early Christians, to be killed for the faith was considered approximating Christ's life and, therefore, perfection. In the middle ages, perfection was approximated by being a hermit, fleeing from the material world, or by joining a religious congregation. I discovered that today, perfection acquires a different meaning. Authentic discipleship today means to choose to be as radical as Jesus, to promote and practice alternative lifestyles, to promote and painstakingly build structures of society which genuinely care for people. It means to live the Gospel, to embrace the cross, and to look forward to the resurrection. It means to make each moment count and waste no efforts, to be intense in one's mission, and yes, to be ready to be persecuted and killed proclaiming one's belief in the Good News that Jesus brings.

July 1988

Kasaysayan ng mga Babaing Kumikibo

ROSARIO BATTUNG, WILHELMINA AT RODOLFO MOLINA

Kababaihan: *Kaisa sa pakikibaka ng mga manggagawa;*
Katuwang sa pagtataguyod ng karapatang
mabuhay na ganap.

Ang kawalan ng kaginhawahan sa pamumuhay na dinaranas ng tao at ang pagtuklas niya na hindi ito kalooban ng Diyos ang siyang nagtutulak sa kanya upang mamulat, maghangad na mahango sa paghihirap, at matutong lumaban para sa kanyang mga karapatan.

Isinasalaysay sa kuwentong ito kung paano nagbago ang anyo at pagtingin ng mga kababaihan na dati'y walang pakialam sa mga pangyayari sa kanilang kapaligiran; kung paano sila namulat at naging aktibo sa pakikibaka para sa karapatang mabuhay na ganap at malaya.

O babaeng walang kibo, magnilay ka at mag-isip;
Malaon ka nang inaapi at malaon ka nang nilulupig.
Bakit hindi ka magtanggol? May anak kang nagugutom,
Bunso mo'y umiiyak, matitiis mo sa hirap;
Ano't hindi ka magbalikwas kung ina kang may
damdamin at paglingap?

Ang kasaysayang ito ay nangyari sa malayong bayang halos di naaabot ng kabihasnan. Malapit ito sa Dagat Pacifico sa kabila ng bundok Sierra Madre. Sa lugar na ito ay may kumpanya ng troso na nagrekrut ng mga tauhan mula sa iba't-ibang lugar. Kaakibat ng pagrekrut ang mga magagandang pangako ng pangasiwaan. Marami sa mga kalalakihan ang nahikayat na magtrabaho sa kumpanya.

Kalaunan ay sumama ang pamamalakad ng pangasiwaan. Tumagal nang kung ilang taong di tumatanggap ng sahod ang mga manggagawa, ngunit tuloy pa rin ang kanilang pagtratrabaho. Paminsan-minsan ay may dumarating na bigas sa kantina at ito ay ipinababale sa mga manggagawa, ngunit kontrolado kung ilan ang ipababale sa bawat manggagawa. Nagtitiis sa ganitong kalagayan ang mga manggagawa sampu ng kanilang mga pamilya, kaya't napilitan silang maghanap ng mauutangan. Ang di pagbibigay ng sahod sa mga manggagawa ang lalong nagpabaon sa kanila sa kahirapan. Nabaon halos ang lahat sa pagkakautang sa iba't-ibang tao; hanggang dumating ang panahong wala nang nagpapautang. Ang pagtitiis ng bawat isa ay umabot na sa sukdulan.

Sa ganitong kalagayan namulat ang mga manggagawa at nakita nila ang pangangailangan ng pagkakaisa para labanan ang may-ari ng kumpanya. Nakita nila ito sa pamamagitan ng pagtatayo ng isang unyon. Ang kahalagahan ng pagkakaisa at pag-uunyon ay nadama ng mga manggagawa. Subalit sa simula ay nahirapan ang mga manggagawa sa pagbubuo ng unyon dahil sinagkaan ito ng kapitalistang may-ari ng kumpanya. Nangako siyang magbibigay ng partial payment sa mga nakabinbing sahod, huwag lamang matuloy ang binabalak na pag-uunyon ng mga manggagawa.

Pumayag ang mga manggagawa at hinintay ang pagsasakatuparan ng mga pangako, ngunit ang lahat ay nanatiling pangakong nakapako. Inabot ng tatlong taon ang nakabinbing sahod ng mga manggagawa. Wala silang maisip na paraan para sa kalutasan ng mga problema; at ito ang nagtulak sa kanila upang muling pagsikapang mabuo ang balak na pag-uunyon. Ito ay nagtagumpay. Naitayo nila ang unyon at nairehistro ito sa Department of Labor and Employment (DOLE).

Nagbalik-tanaw ang mga manggagawa at ang kanilang maybahay sa kasaysayan ng kanilang unyon: "Nagsikap kaming magkaisa noon, ngunit takot kami. Nagkaisa na lang kami noong naging `mulat kami sa katotohanan.' Nalaman namin na ang aming ipinaglalaban ay makataru-ngan at batay sa kalooban ng Diyos. Dahil dito ang mga balak naming pagbabago ng kalagayan ay di lamang nina-nais ng iilan sa amin. Parami nang parami ang aming bilang hanggang sa ang lahat ay kasama na sa pagkilos at pagpapatupad ng lahat ng aming mga balak. Nagkaroon kami ng mga repleksyon sa ugnayan ng aming buhay at ng aming pananampalataya. Batay ito sa aming patuloy na pag-aaral sa aming partikular na kalagayan na iniuugnay namin sa kalagayan ng malawak na lipunan; repleksyon sa Bibliya; sama-samang panalangin; at sama-samang pagkilos para sa pagbabago ng sarili at sitwasyon namin at ng bayan."

Nakaabot sila sa ganitong pagkakaisa sa pahakbang-hakbang na paraan. Ngunit di lahat ng kanilang hakbang ay matagumpay.

Nagpetisyon ang mga manggagawa sa Presidente ng Pilipinas at sa DOLE. Tumugon ang may-ari ng kumpanya at nagbigay ng partial payment sa di pa nabayarang sahod. Di ito tinanggap ng mga manggagawa sapagkat ang kanilang kahilingan ay ibigay ang buong sahod at di lamang partial payment.

Nagkaroon ng hidwaan ang mga mag-aasawa dahil sa magkaibang pagtingin sa problema. Ang pagtingin ng mga maybahay ay mas mabuti nang tanggapin ang partial pay-ment kaysa walang matanggap. Ang tingin naman ng mga kalalakihan ay dapat ibigay ang buong sahod dahil ito'y kulang pa ngang pambayad sa lahat ng pagkakautang. Hindi pa nakikita ng mga kababaihan sa panahong ito ang kahalagahan ng pagkakaisa, at ang nasa isip lamang nila ay kung paano mapapakain ang mga anak at mabubuhay ang kanilang mga pamilya. Napilitang tanggapin ng mga manggagawa ang inaalok na sahod, at panandaliang naging normal ang takbo ng kanilang buhay.

Naantala na naman ang pagbigay ng natitirang sahod, kayat humantong na ang pagkilos ng mga manggagawa sa pagtigil sa trabaho o welga. Ang pangasiwaan ay nangako na naman ngunit naging matatag na rito ang mga manggagawa. Dahil sa mga pangyayari ay namulat na rin ang mga maybahay sa mga panloloko at pagsasamantalang ginagawa ng may-ari ng kumpanya. Nakita nila na ang may-ari ay di tumitingin para sa kagalingan ng mga manggagawa at ng kanilang mga pamilya, ngunit sa halip ay tinatrato panga silang parang mga busabos at alipin. Naunawaan din nila kung bakit ganoon na lamang ang paghahangad ng kanilang mga asawa na makapagtayo ng unyon at makuha ng buo ang kanilang sahod... na ito ay para sa kagalingan ng buong pamilya. Dahil sila rin ang humahawak ng pera at nagbabadyet para sa pang-araw-araw na gastusin, nadama nila ang bigat at ang sobrang paghihikahos sa buhay. Naging aktibo ang mga maybahay sa pagsubaybay sa lahat ng pagkilos ng unyon. Nakita nila ang pagkakaisa sa kanilang mga asawa.

Ang kawalan ng kaginhawaan sa buhay na dinaranas ng tao ...

Dahil dito nagkaisa ang mga maybahay na magbuo ng samahan. Gumawa sila ng isang paninindigan na susuporta sa lahat ng pagkilos na gagawin ng unyon laban sa pagmamalabis ng kapitalista, at bilang pagtulong sa paghahanap ng ibang ikabubuhay sa panahon ng welga. Ang samahan ay tinawag nilang *Samahan ng mga Babaeng Kumikibo*. Hangad ng mga kasapi nito ang pagbabago at ang pagkawala sa miserableng pamumuhay. Binubuo ang kanilang samahan ng humigit kumulang sa 50 kababaihan na pawang mga maybahay ng mga manggagawa. Naninindigan ang grupo na itataguyod ang suporta sa pakikibaka ng mga manggagawa laban sa kapitalista. Nanindigan din sila upang kumilos para sa panggigiit ng kanilang karapatan bilang tao at bilang mga babae, at ng kanilang karapatang mabuhay nang ganap.

Ang unang pagkilos na nilahukan ng kababaihan ay ang paggawa ng liham na nagpapaabot ng kanilang mga hinaing at problema sa DOLE at sa Pangulo ng Pilipinas.

Natuklasan nilang wala palang nangyari sa kanilang pagkilos sapagkat wala man lamang naging tulong o tugong nagmula sa gobyerno. Hindi binigyan ng aksyon ang naipaabot nilang problema at kalagayan ng mga manggagawa. Sa halip na pilitin ang may-ari na magbayad ng sahod, nag-issue pa ang pamahalaan ng back-to-work order sa mga manggagawa.

... ang nagtutulak sa kanya upang lumaban para sa kanyang mga karapatan

Bilang sagot ay gumawa uli ng liham ang mga maybahay na ipinadala sa DOLE. Ang liham ay nagtanong kung bakit kailangang pabalikin sa trabaho ang mga manggagawa samantalang di pa nagbabayad ng utang sa sahod ang kapitalista. Ngunit tulad ng dapat asahan, di na naman binigyan ng pansin ang naturang liham.

Umabot sa sukdulan ang pangyayari. Tuluyang nagsara ang kumpanya at di na nabayaran ang mga manggagawa. Dahil dito, nagkaisa ang mga manggagawa sampu ng kanilang maybahay na kumpiskahin at ipagbili ang mga kagamitan ng kumpanya kung saan ang kikitain ay paghahatian nilang lahat. Hinadlangan ito ng mga tagapagbantay ng kumpanya, ngunit hindi ito nakapigil sa pagkuha ng mga gamit. Humantong ang pangyayari sa pamahalaang bayan. Nagsampa ng kaso sa huwes ang pangasiwaan. Ang kaso ay pagnanakaw dahil ang mga kagamitan ay hindi pag-aari ng mga kumuha. Pinadalhan ng subpoena ang ilang opisyales ng unyon. Bilang pagpapakita ng pagkakaisa, sumamang lahat ang mga manggagawa pati na ang kanilang mga maybahay sa korte. Sinabi nila sa huwes, "Karapatan naming kunin ang lahat ng mga kagamitang iyan dahil *karapatan namin bilang tao ang mabuhay.* Ang aming kinuha ay sa amin dahil di nila binayaran ang aming pinagtrabahuhan. Kulang pa nga kung tutuusin ang lahat ng iyan sa tagal ng aming naranasang paghihirap at pagtitiis kung saan ay halos minsan na lang kami kumain sa isang araw." Walang nagawa ang huwes kundi ang magpahayag na balewala ang kaso laban sa mga manggagawa.

Sa kabila ng lahat ng mga pangyayari, ang katanungang bumabagabag sa damdamin ng mga kababaihan ay kung hanggang kailan tatagal ang lahat ng ito? Saan uli kukuha ng ikabubuhay ang bawat isa?

Nagplano ang grupo kung ano ang hakbang na dapat gawin sa ganitong kalagayan. Napagkaisahan nila na ipagpatuloy ang paninindigan, ang pagkakaisa, ang pagtulong at pagsuporta sa bawat isa, at ang pagkilos upang mabuhay ang pamilya. Ginugol nila ang panahon sa pagpapaunlad ng kabuhayan sa pamamagitan ng pagtatanim ng mga gulay, prutas at lamang-ugat tulad ng kamote, ube, gabi, at iba pang puwedeng maging kapalit ng bigas. Nagtulungan sila sa paghawan ng lupa upang siyang pagtataniman. Sapagkat matagal pang panahon bago mapakinabangan ang tanim, pinasok nila ang pagluluto ng asin mula sa tubig dagat. Tiniis nila ang ganitong mahirap na gawain dahil na rin sa paghahangad na mabuhay. Natuto rin ang mga kababaihang mangisda at ipagpalit ito sa bigas ng ibang baryo. Naging pinakapangunahing ikabubuhay ng buong pamilya ang pagluluto ng asin. Kahit mapapakinabangan lamang ito pagkatapos ng isang linggong pag-iigib ng tubig-dagat at panggatong sa buong magdamag at maghapon, nakakasiguro naman sila nang may maipagbibili at maipagpapalit para sa kanilang mga pangangailangan. Hindi naging regular ang pangingisda dahil nakadepende ito sa takbo ng panahon.

Lumahok din ang grupo ng kababaihan sa ilang pangkulturang pagtatanghal, sa pagsasadula ng kanilang buhay mula sa matagal na di pagkibo tungo sa pagkagising, paki-kibaka at pakikipaglaban para sa buhay. Naging aktibo rin sila sa mga usaping pangkalusugan ng baryo. Lumahok sila sa mga programa ng simbahan ukol sa kalusugan. Natuto sila ng pag-alam ng sakit ng tao, paggamot sa sakit, at pagpapaliwanag kung paano maiiwasan ang sakit. Patuloy ang kanilang repleksyon sa kanilang mga pagkilos, kung saan naiuugnay nila ang buhay sa kanilang pananampalataya.

Upang maipagpatuloy ang pagpapatibay ng kanilang pagkakaisa, ang mga bumuo ng mga nabuwag na unyon at ang samahan ng mga kababaihan ay nagsanib at nagtayo ng *Samahan ng mga Mag-uuway*. Magkakatulong silang lahat sa pagtataguyod ng layunin para sa pagbabago at paggigiit ng kanilang mga karapatan. Nagpuputol sila ng uway mula sa gubat at iniipon ito upang sama-samang ibi-biyahe at ipagbibili. Ito ngayon ang napagkukunan nila ng ikabubuhay.

Dahil na rin sa pagsasamantala ng mga mamimili ng uway sa murang halaga, nagkaisa ang grupo na ipunin ang nakuhang uway at sila na mismo ang magbebenta sa ibang lugar sa mas mataas na presyo. Nagtayo rin sila ng isang tindahan na pansamantalang tutugon sa kanilang mga pangangailangan habang di pa naibebenta ang mga uway. Ang kooperatibang ito ay di nagtagumpay dahil sa kaku-langan sa pinansya. Sinubukan din nilang maglunsad ng isang proyekto sa paggawa ng rattan furnitures na gagamit ng uway na nakukuha nila sa gubat.

Lahat ng kanilang pagsisikap ay hindi nagtagumpay dahil sa sobrang paghihigpit ng mga nanunungkulan. Kung sino pa ang nagpapakahirap upang magkaroon lamang ng kakainin ay sila pa ang nasisilip at hinihigpitan. Samantalang ang mga mayayamang nakaupo lamang at naghihintay ng aakyat na kabuhayan ang siya pang niluluwagan. Pinagbintangan pang isang subersibong organisas-yon ang Samahan dahil hindi ito umaayon sa kagustuhan ng mga maykapangyarihan.

Sa kabila ng krisis ay nagpatuloy ang samahan sa loob ng dalawang taon. Ang mga indibidwal na bumubuo nito ay pinaghinalaan at pinagbintangang mga subersibo. Hinuli at inaresto ang karamihan sa kanila. Sinubukang harapin ito ng samahan ngunit tuminding lubha ang sitwasyon. Wala silang nagawa at dahil sa kanilang pag-iwas ay nagkahiwa-hiwalay ang grupo. Nagkanya-kanya sila nang paghahanap ng lugar na mapasisimulan ng panibagong buhay, kung saan makakapagpatuloy ng bagong anyo ng pakikibaka.

Ang mga bintang at kahirapang dinanas nila ay hindi naging sagka upang maipagpatuloy nila ang kanilang pag-kilos at maipaglaban ang kanilang karapatang mabuhay bilang mga tao at di bilang mga hayop na sunud-sunuran sa utos ng amo. Nabuwag man ang samahang nabuo, nakatiim na sa isipan ng bawat kasapi ang mga simulain at prinsipyo nito.

Hangga ngayon, saan man sila mapadako, nagpapa-tuloy pa rin sila sa pakikibaka para sa karapatang mabuhay na ganap at malaya. Kabilang ang marami sa kanila sa mga organisadong grupo at batayang pamayanan. May ilan na sa kanila ang nagbuwis ng buhay para sa ganap na pagbabago at sa pagkamit ng tunay na kalayaan.

EDITORS' TRANSLATION:

From Passivity to Committed Action:
A Story of Women's Struggle

The absence of basic living comforts and the realization that this is not God's will force people to open their eyes, to long for alleviation from poverty, and to learn to fight for their rights.

This is a story of how women rose from passivity and indifference to active participation in the struggle for their right to lead full and free lives. It is a story of struggling men and women in a town hardly reached by civilization, near the mountains of the Sierra Madre.

> Oh passive woman
> Think and reflect
> You've long been oppressed
> You've long been abused
> Why don't you defend yourself?
> You have a child starving to death
> Your youngest child cries in pain
> Can you bear to keep them in suffering and anguish?
> As a concerned mother feeling compassion
> Why don't you liberation you liberate yourself
> and your sisters and all from bondage? [1]

In this remote town was a logging company which exploited its workers no end. Poor working conditions, low and often delayed wages, and the company's indifference to their grievances led the workers to form a union. At first, management promised the union partial payment of three years' back wages. The wives of the workers convinced their husbands to take the offer of management. All that mattered to them at this point was to ease in some way their families' economic hardship, as they were the ones who

---

[1] Translation by the authors.

had to budget the measly earnings of their husbands. After much debate, the workers finally accepted management's offer. The management, however, did not keep its promise. This forced the union to stage a strike.

The broken promises of management and worsening working conditions led the women to form their own organization to support their husbands. In the beginning they were just plain housewives faithful to their traditional roles of housekeeping and mothering their children. For sometime, they remained bystanders and dissuaded their husbands from participating in collective union actions. They had such a near-sighted view of their extremely exploited situation which they passively accepted and negatively fostered.

As they reflected on the reality of their situation, they realized that all the hardships they bore were not willed by God. They discovered and were empowered by the knowledge that God wills the triumph of their struggle for justice. They realized that their misery will continue if they will not participate directly in the struggle of the workers. They were also beginning to understand the connection between the problems they face in their homes with the problems of the workers in the company.

Their unity as a women's group was gradually forged. Their undertakings had some successes and many failures. They wrote letters to the President and to the Department of Labor and Employment to pressure the company to heed their demands. Government authorities, however, did not listen to their grievances and instead gave them a back-to-work order.

The conflict between management and the workers worsened, until the company finally closed down. The workers never received their back wages. They and their families then confiscated and sold the company's properties. They divided the proceeds among themselves. The company in turn filed a case of robbery against them. The workers and their wives stood on a united position that they earned the profits they got from selling the properties out of years of unpaid labor. The court could not deny the justness of the workers' action and finally dismissed the case against them.

With the closure of the company, they were forced to venture into other sources of livelihood. The women went into fishing, salt-making, vegetable planting and land cultivation. Their husbands, meanwhile, gathered rattan from the forests which they sold to small entrepreneurs. All their efforts, however, miserably failed because of various restrictions imposed by government agencies.

The women's groups continued their activities. They held cultural activities essaying their experience from silence to awakening and struggle. They engaged in community health programs. They continued their reflections where they were able to relate their faith to their life experiences.

The women and the rattan-gatherers, mostly former members of the disbanded workers' union, banded together and formed a new organization. The group was later on suspected of being subversive. Most of its members were arrested. After two years, the organization was disbanded. The members were forced to evacuate their homes and migrate to different places.

Now, despite the disbandment of their group and their separation from one another, they still strive to continue their struggle in their own localities. The visions they once shared are permanently implanted in their consciousness and will continue to move them to action, wherever they may be.

"When Others Are Shedding Blood, What Right Have I To Shed Tears?"

EVELYN BALAIS-SERRANO

My involvement and concern for human rights started during the early martial law years when I was almost arrested while doing organizing work among the urban poor of Tondo. Then as a social worker, I joined the campaign for the release of detained colleagues of the Philippine Association of Social Workers (PASW). I became wife of a political prisoner for four years before the February revolution, afterwhich I joined the Task Force Detainees of the Philippines (TFDP) as a human rights worker.

My first actual experience in human rights work was with TFDP when it was organized in 1974 by the Association of Major Religious Superiors in response to the increasing number of political prisoners. As a student volunteer of TFDP, I was tasked to visit detainees and document their cases. At that time, people who do this kind of work were considered leftists or communists. With other volunteers, we would keep our work a secret even from our parents and teachers because we knew they would not allow us to continue this work. After graduation, some of my classmates opted to stay with TFDP while I was offered a scholarship for my masteral degree abroad. I decided to try organizing work in Tondo instead.

It was the height of the urban poor's struggle for land against the then First Lady's whim of transforming the area into an international port. We held a series of seminars and meetings to study the issues involved and to prepare the people to negotiate with the authorities. The people were angered and frightened when some of the leaders of ZOTO, the leading organization, were arrested and detained during one big mobilization. I remember how the military were rounding up the areas almost every night, chasing the community organizers and leaders. Twice or thrice, we were almost caught. We would go to the areas during the day and sleep somewhere else during the night. It was like playing hide and seek with the military. We knew that if we were caught, we'd rot in jail because we would be detained indefinitely without any charges whatsoever. Except perhaps if we have good connections in the Government, which we didn't have. I learned from the other organizers that the training coordinator of our program was imprisoned for three years. I never thought I would marry this man more than a year later.

I met Gani after he was released. Seven months later, we were married. He was severely tortured upon his arrest and his long detention seriously affected him. He seemed to be always running after time, trying hard to make up for the missed opportunities while in prison. Often he was restless and tense. He smoked like a chimney. It was difficult for me to cope and adjust. During this time, I was doing full-time work among farmers in Central Luzon while he worked in Metro Manila, a rather difficult arrangement, but somehow we managed.

With the coming of my second baby, I had to give up my organizing work to attend to my then sickly child. From the countryside, we transferred to the city where I settled for an office-based job with the PASW. It wasn't easy because I already conditioned myself to work with the grassroot farmers. I welcomed the idea though because it would mean being with my husband more often and establishing a more or less "normal" family life.

But not for long. Gani was re-arrested during the labor crackdown in September 1982. For another four years, he was in prison. These were my most trying years. Looking back, I felt I myself was in prison. Physically, I was not a captive. But my mind, my heart, my soul were confined in Camp Crame.

Worse, I was being harassed by the military. They perhaps suspected that I have documents which could be used as evidence against my husband. I would be followed by plainclothesmen in my trips, guarded in my office, and called up in the phone at unholy hours of the day. I used to tremble at the very sight of these hard-faced men. I imagined myself being raped and the thought of it made me vomit. Then I would see their faces in my dreams. I had sleepless nights, and days when I could hardly eat. On several instances, I would miss the street where we live while riding on a jeepney or tricycle on my way home.

*I met the bravest women
in my life ... mothers and wives, some
of whom lost their husbands, sons and
daughters, but still struggling ...
I felt ashamed that I had
to cry a lot about my
own situation*

There was an instance when a red car stopped by my side on my way home from the camp. The door sprung open: "Come, ride in, I know where you're going." "Why will I? I don't even know you," I managed to say. I continued walking. The car moved as I moved, almost touching my side. After a few meters, the door opened again. "Come on, don't be hard-headed!" I tried to cross the street. It maneuvered and continued following me. After a while it drove forward and blocked my way. As the man inside alighted, I saw some relatives of detainees coming. I shouted at them and ran towards their direction. I almost collapsed when I reached them, frightened at the thought of what could possibly have happened to me if I was forcibly taken by that time.

At the time of Gani's detention, Toni, my eldest, and Karl were only four and two years old respectively. We were surviving on my meager allowance and some help from friends. I realized that my children were more affected than I was. My daughter would stare blankly on the walls of her classroom and suddenly would break into tears without any provocation. At times, she would not go to school. My son, on the other hand, would be sick most of the time whenever we would leave the detention camp after week-end visits. Until now, whenever there are threats or actual instances of long separation or disappearance, he usually gets sick.

One of the difficulties I had was how to answer their questions: *"Bakit kinulong si Tats?* (Tats is short for Tatay), *Kinukulong ba talaga ang mabait? Bakit tinotortyur ang* detainees? *Bingi ba ang Diyos? Bakit ang dami-dami ko nang dasal hindi pa rin Niya naririnig? Iba ba ang Diyos ni Marcos? Salbahe ba ang Diyos niya? Ilang tulog pa bago lumaya? Ilang Pasko pa? Ilang birthday ko pa...?* Endless questions. How would I explain so they would understand? One time I heard the two kids arguing on what to do with Marcos because of what he did to their father. "I'd throw him in the sea and feed him to the sharks," said the boy.

"No, put him in jail and let the ants eat and bite him together with his wife," insisted the girl. Somehow, I tried to answer them in the most precise and candid way I know. I realized later that they understood because whenever they are asked by friends, they would answer exactly as I did.

In those four years, I was a member of KAPATID, the organization of relatives and friends of detainees. It was there where I met the mothers, the wives, the sisters and children of long-time prisoners. We would tell stories of our loved ones. We would cry. Then we would also laugh at our funny experiences in following up the cases of our detained kins. We used to follow up the cases individually. However, some of the wives, sisters and daughters were being sexually harassed and abused by some military men. We then decided to go in groups, which proved to be more effective.

In my integration with other detainees and families, I realized I was not alone. I felt even lucky because my situation was much better than most others. Their problem was more of survival: where to get their next meal, how to go about the children's schooling, and others. I felt ashamed that I had to cry a lot about my own situation. I felt weak about my commitment. I came face to face with mothers and wives, some of whom lost their husbands, sons and daughters, but still firmly struggling and ever committed. It was there where I met the bravest women in my life, simple and practical, strong and determined.

Camp Crame was horrifying for me. I felt like being raped everytime the guards search my body and my things upon entering and leaving the cells. I felt worse than a prostitute everytime we paid our conjugal visits. In my four years of working for my husband's release, my only dream then was for him to get out of that hell, so I could also be

released. I visited him every week-end without fail, except when I left for Canada and the US to attend a conference and to visit my family at the death of my father.

I went to Canada and the US mainly to campaign for the release of colleague Judy Taguiwalo. Judy was detained while she was pregnant. She gave birth to and brought up her child in prison. She was held in the same camp my husband was in. After talking about her case among colleagues from different countries, I would say, "By the way, my husband is also a political detainee."

In one program in the US, the opening number was a song entitled "Kalayaan." I was so touched, I cried. The singer, looking at me, could not continue singing because she too started crying. After a while, almost everyone in the audience was crying. At the end of the program, practically everyone gave something for the detainees: a book, a shirt, a chain, a card, and quite a lot of money. The most touching was the many pledges of support to campaign for their release.

Gani and the other detainees' release after the February revolution was a dream come true. After our continuous vigil at the gates of Camp Crame, trying to get in to see how they were during the time the "revolution" was going on, they were finally freed upon the new president's order.

With more than 600 prisoners released, TFDP hired me to set up a national program for direct services to the ex-detainees and their families, including those prisoners still detained in jail. We set up a pilot rehabilitation center in Metro Manila and systematized its operation. During one of my visits to a nearby provincial jail, I found the prison condition terribly suffocating: no light, no air, no water, no facilities. The detainees were padlocked in their cells like sardines in a can.

I blurted, "How can you bear this kind of situation? This is a violation of your rights!" One of them answered, "We're used to this kind of life. In fact, it's even better here because even if the food is sometimes spoiled, at least we are assured we will have something to eat." Another spoke, "What we cannot stomach is the fact that we are here because we believe in something good." I almost cried, not for pity but anger. As I sat there listening to their stories, bathing with perspiration, I thought, how can one talk of human rights here when throughout their lives their rights are being denied?

I remember whenever the ex-Crame detainees would have those rare chances of seeing each other, they would wish they were in prison again because they felt more secure there. They have food to eat, place to sleep, with free water and electricity. They would even joke that they have the luxury of having guards twenty-four hours a day.

Recently, a father of a salvaged victim from Southern Luzon was referred to me. He showed me right away the colored picture of her daughter. She was very young and very lovely. She was killed by the military, and he wanted to get her body but did not know how. He looked very worried. I found out after a while that he was apprehensive about what the military would ask him when he claims the body. He was afraid that they might also take his three-year old son and use the child as a hostage to force him to surrender.

His apprehensions were quite valid because there were similar cases where a wife was detained because the military were after the husband. We had a long talk. He was more relaxed and feeling better when he finally bid goodbye. A couple of weeks later, the victim's body was exhumed and buried in Metro Manila. Her body was deformed, apparently as a result of severe torture and foul play.

My few meetings with the father inspired me a lot. Such a courageous man! He was obviously hiding his tears but I could very well feel his pain inside. The way he talked about his daughter showed his tremendous respect for her and her comrades. Until now, as I look at the daughter's picture on my table, I could feel her warmth and sweetness, her courage and determination, just like her father.

She reminded me of Puri Pedro, a close friend and colleague who was also killed by the military. When I heard the news, I could not eat nor sleep for days. I could imagine her being raped several times by different men, being tied to her neck and hanged till she died. She was so young and so much alive!

And Susan, a classmate whom I personally encouraged to work with the farmers. And Rose, a social work student and a best friend. Both were mercilessly killed by the military. And then there were Ka Lando, Lean; and every now and then we learn of Gani's fellow detainees' and friends' disappearances, attempted assassinations, arrests, torture, detention.

Everytime I am confronted with such cases, I feel a part of me dies. I feel a certain emptiness that leaves me reflecting for days. How many more lives? How many more widows and orphans? How long shall we wait? How long shall we fight? But when I meet the mothers, the widows, the sons and daughters, I feel alive again. In their grief and sorrow, they protest and they fight. How many widows are now taking up the cause of their slain husbands? How many mothers consider their slain or missing children's friends and comrades their own children?

I am at a point when I can say I am no longer afraid. I still tremble at the sight of the military. I still have this "Cramephobia." I still cry a lot when I hear stories of victims. I still panic when I hear about coups. But I feel I can take almost anything, anyhow. I know I would always tremble, I would always have the phobia, and I would always cry and panic, but not anymore because of fear but because of anger and protest and the firm resolve that something must be done.

The Struggle for Human Rights: Beyond Vigilance

ADORA FAYE DE VERA

I was arrested and detained without charges at the age of seventeen, a few months after the declaration of Martial Law. At that time, Government officials were praising national security to high heavens, and the whole print and broadcast media started to forget how many innocent people were killed in Mendiola, Plaza Miranda or Corregidor just months before. Reliable newspapers were muzzled. All organizations except those controlled by the Government were banned. The critical thinking and outspokenness that marked our activism was left for the fledgling student movement to sustain. Amid the spreading fear and intensifying repression, we conducted secret study groups and issued statements (which were never picked up by the press) — activities that became more and more dangerous as the military machinery consolidated power into its hands.

The value our society gave to human rights at the early period of Martial Law can be measured in how quickly the combination of police action and government propaganda was able to spread fear among the people throughout the urban centers; how quickly relatives and friends started convincing activists to give Marcos and his "new society" a chance, despite all the restrictions imposed on their own freedom. This also indicated a method of coping, following obnoxious rules when people feel too powerless to resist.

The right to freedom and opinion and expression. The right to be free from arbitrary arrest, detention or exile. The right to be given a fair and public hearing; to be presumed innocent until proven guilty. These words became faint echoes of a bill of rights someone studied somewhere in secondary school. By the time intelligence operatives started slapping socks at my face to make me "confess about my subversive activities," I was already conscious of the risk activism entailed in a militarized society. Torture to me was no longer a personal assault, just something to bear with, something that would pass after which I could be active in the movement again.

For the next several years, I lived in the countryside, planting crops with the peasants and helping them get organized. It was here where I witnessed farmers being dispersed by military gunfire just because they formed mutual aid organizations. It was here where I saw how children could become malnourished yet stay alive; how inaccessible health centers and schools were. It was here where I saw how women got old and toothless at the age of twenty-five because of too much work and too little food and rest; how they could be beaten, forced into marriages, and forbidden to make decisions concerning work animals; how they could not talk about the rape and abuse they suffered from their husbands or landlords; how we had to ask permission from the men just so they would allow their wives to be organized.

Life among peasants gave me some clues on why Martial Law succeeded and failed. It became effective at its inception because, for the majority of Filipinos like us, freedom never existed anyway, and a new name for a new regime did not make much of a difference. We never really had a chance to take part in the government, unless we consider guns and bribes as our representatives. The rights to just and favorable conditions of work, to protection against unemployment, to equal pay for equal work, to just and favorable renumeration for labor, were all rights that continued to sleep on paper because multinational corporations just had more access to these rights than we did. And the rights to education, to an adequate standard of living, to rest and leisure, were unknown luxuries in an agrarian society where one who controls the land controls our lives as well. For all the terror it meant to inspire, Martial Law was just something to bear with, something that would pass, afterwhich we could go on with our lives.

The struggle for human rights requires not just vigilance, but militance

I was arrested and detained without charges again in 1976 because of my work with peasants. By this time, the phenomenon of involuntary disappearances started to emerge. I was spirited away to a military safehouse and subjected to intermittent physical, psychological and sexual torture. I was subject to my captors' every whim, dead to the outside world. I got out of prison after nine months of living death, only to enter a larger prison. A price was immediately placed on my head, so I went into hiding, unable to visit my son for more than five years.

Martial Law ceased to be just another "new society." Amid the deteriorating economic conditions and the growing restlessness of the population, the military machinery was running amok, contributing to the fast-rising death toll of innocent people. It was this situation that aroused people to act in defense of their lives. The people's movement against fascism started to gain momentum, supported by a growing peasant movement in the countryside.

Working with the peasant women, consoling the widows and children of farmers who died from strafing, becoming part of village relays to warn people of approaching military formations, I realized what we all had in common — we were fighting for our right to live. In so doing, we were able to recognize all our other rights as well.

Such was the nature of the movement that finally brought an end to Martial Law. It was a movement that sought to recover not only formal political rights lost to martial rule but all other rights inherent in human beings, including those hitherto not experienced but now realizable by the people's organized force. We were no longer powerless.

Martial Law was formally lifted in 1981 and the Marcos regime was deposed in 1986. We considered them major victories for the human rights movement. But too soon, a number of our people from the middle class started becoming complacent, satisfied with the democratic forms they saw being restored — forms that already existed before martial law but did not prove effective enough to prevent it. Some of them even went to the extent of subverting people's demands, twisting the meaning of human rights to accommodate their political interests.

Meanwhile, even as a new government is in place, Filipinos at the grassroots continue to struggle for basic survival — truly the survival of the nation as a whole — from foreign economic and military interests that threaten to choke us to death. The struggling grassroots continue to be exposed to great risks in the face of intensified militarism and militarization. More and more women, children and elderly are falling prey to human rights violations. Can we claim victory with these developments?

As long as human rights advocacy is perceived as representing far-off, idealized standards of freedom and international solidarity peripheral to our people's struggle for survival, it will remain a middle class movement dependent upon intimations of democratic facades and media hype. The struggle for human rights will be relevant only to our people if it furthers their struggle as workers, as peasants, as women, as fisherfolk. The struggle for human rights in a Third World country such as ours goes beyond the signing and popularization of articles and provisions on human rights. It implies taking part in the struggle to change socio-political structures that make the exercise of these rights possible. The struggle for human rights requires not just vigilance, but militance.

Massacres, arrests and orchestrated anti-people propaganda suggest an eerie pattern of a program already implemented before. Today, however, it has an alarming difference. Bombings, massive evacuations and mutilation of corpses seem to be "improvements" to the original model. There is no formal declaration of martial rule, but this is more than compensated for by continued reference to national security and the protection of a democracy we supposedly won. These are familiar patterns with updated versions. Will we respond the way we did before?

Our experience of martial rule gave us deeper understanding about the instruments of state control. We now have a strong people's movement that is slowly making our dreams realizable. Even if women activists leave for work everyday half-expecting to come home to a ransacked apartment or to a waiting car with no plate numbers, it is not with resignation to the unbearable rules of the game. It is with determination to fight for our rights.

Working again with women after my third arrest, I am glad to know myself more as a human rights advocate than as a victim of human rights violations. One day, I asked a peasant woman what impact our struggles had on her. She replied, *"Naging tao ako. Maraming bahagi na ng buhay ko ang kaya kong pagpasyahan. At kaya ko ring ipaglaban ang mga bahaging hindi pa."* (I became more human. There are now more parts of my life that I can control. And I can fight for those that I still can't.) That, I believe, is what our work for human rights is all about.

The Faces of Human Rights Violations I See

Joy Hofer

I will never forget my feelings that evening in Guatemala City as I sat with the wife of my doctor. She was mourning her husband's death at the hands of a death squad. The day before, armed men approached his pick-up while he was driving his three children to school. They asked his identity and then calmly held a revolver to his head and pulled the trigger. Jumping on the back of the pick-up they sprayed gunfire on the cab. The children survived, but forever scarred by the memory.

I drove down the mountainside numbed by what I heard and saw. As I looked at the twinkling lights of slums I thought of the thousands of families who share this raw terror and sorrow without a name.

There would be no investigation, no charges brought against the killers of the doctor. The papers would report that he was assassinated by "unknowns." For the thousands without money there would be no articles on the front pages, no investigations, no charges. Every month 300 people meet their death this way during my time in Guatemala.

That evening I personally felt what human rights violations meant to the victims. I remember the sick feeling in my stomach; the helplessness and the fear that the next moment the fragile shell of what we assume was stable reality would suddenly shatter and I would be swept into a sickening hole where people were tortured, illegally detained in clandestine prisons, and then would mysteriously "disappear" without their families ever knowing what happened to them.

What made the death of the doctor so shocking, so emotionally devastating for me was that he was a human being.

The word "human" is central to "human rights violations." Every human has a soul, something sacred, something that puts her or him beyond the world of objects. A human rights violation is an act of irreverence, a desecration. We feel devastation and hopelessness when there are human rights violations because such violations strike at the center of what being human is all about.

The resulting chaos, fear and helplessness that the act of violation spawns on the victim's friends, family and colleagues provide a convenient opportunity for the state to flex its oppressive power of control. That is why it is such a powerful weapon in the hands of a repressive state.

During my time in Central America I began to understand that human rights violations went far beyond the countless assassinations of professors, doctors, lawyers, journalists, peasants, church workers, labor organizers and health workers that were sensationally reported in the dailies.

At first it was easy to assume that the men in uniforms, toting machine guns and packed on the back of half-ton trucks were the main human rights violators. They were mostly poor Indians forcibly recruited or practically kidnaped into serving in the army.

The shock troops of this army, the biggest and strongest men and dressed in camouflage, were fearfully referred to as the *pintadas*, the painted ones. I heard dreadful stories of their training: being forced to eat live chickens with bare hands and being forbidden to have any contact with their families for months on end. They were brainwashed to believe that their own people — their mothers, children, cousins, girlfriends — were the enemy, "communists" who deserve to die as animals, or worse.

I remember my terror as I saw the soldiers' blank faces with eyes that never "saw" farther than the surface. Where was their soul, their spirit? Were they human any more? Were they something else? How could they carry out such grotesque orders? I could only see them as "enemy," to be stopped at all costs. Over time I began to realize that the soldiers, the obvious enemy, are also a violated people.

What do these reflections have to do with my life in the Philippines today? I still get that sick feeling in my stomach when I hear of a "salvaged" worker. "Salvaging" is the Philippine equivalent of death at the hands of a death squad. Salvaging does not seem as intense here as in Central America, but everywhere the threat, the darkness of what happens when the evil of human rights violations gets strong, is always a shadow, a fear that grips the heart.

How shall we respond as Christians? We stand on the side of life, spirit, and the humanity of all. We stand against death, violation and the desecration of all human beings.

The challenge is to recognize all victims of human rights abuses, not only the Ninoy Aquinos, the Steve Bikos and the Archbishop Oscar Romeros. Not even just the peasants in Negros whose houses are burnt, or the industrial workers who are salvaged, or the health workers who are threatened by anti-communist vigilante groups. We need to see the human rights of hungry children in the slums of Manila, the farmers without enough land to feed their families, the peasant child killed in an AFP-NPA encounter.

Human rights violations include hunger, unemployment, landlessness, unavailability of schools and health services. The violations are deep within the structures of our societies. They occur more often than the dramatic moment when a slum organizer is pulled out from a jeepney by armed men for interrogation. The violations happen every night when a mother has to quiet a hungry child; when a school-age Muslim boy must beg on the streets; or when a farmer has only three bags of rice left after harvest for his family of ten.

My role in these crimes is not always clear. I walk by and rationalize over my simple lifestyle when I pay for groceries, or when I refuse to look in the eyes of a beggar woman with two sickly children by her side.

As Christians we are called to stand and listen to the stories of these people. The story of Yahweh asking Cain where his brother is is our story. "The blood of your brothers and sisters cries from the earth. Where are they?" God asks.

May 1988

World Issues Trickle Down...
To the Slums of Leveriza

Christine Tan

It is relatively simple for us who are victims of a fourteen-year Marcos totalitarian regime to write about human rights violations. We only need to recall the cases of arbitrary arrests, the massacres and ambushes, the tortures and "salvaging," the forced and false testimonies, and the mock military trials or sham hearings of a gagged Supreme Court. A number of our acquaintances until today are still missing, perhaps dead, leaving anguish and darkness to mothers, wives and sweethearts. Life in our country still brims with such aching experiences.

At this instance, however, I choose to tell the stories of other people. Among the shanties of Bombay, the squatters of Manila, or along the *klongs* of Bangkok and the *sampans* of Hong Kong, a staggering mass of nameless poor suffers daily and without respite from the violence of human rights violations. Such raw injustice attracts no press coverage or prestigious fact-finding missions. Because they are generally unrecognized by the public, they are endured by their victims and taken for granted by those who, like the Levite in the Bible, pass them by.

For almost ten years now, a small group of Catholic Sisters, to which I belong, is living with 25,000 Filipinos in an urban slum in the heart of Manila. In the beginning, it was the high density of persons and things that shattered our sensibilities. We would not accept the reality of seeing a family of fourteen people sleeping, eating, squatting and doing everything else in a four meter by four meter shack; or watch three mothers, each about to deliver a child, lie in labor on the same cot; of people walking along pathways lined by hills of garbage on both sides.

We were not accustomed to pass by drains and sewers clogged with the debris of decades, or galvanized cement, and dead cats decomposing. Neither were we immune to the excitement of spotting thirty-nine grown men jump into a jeep and balance themselves on its roof, steps, sides and seats.

The woeful lack or absence of the basic creations of God is another aspect of this urban misery. Who said that the best things in life are free? By three o'clock every morning, pails, drums, gasoline cans stand in line, waiting to be filled up with water from a lone faucet.

Once, during a field trip to a mountain spot, a little boy, Irwin, after playing around for hours, grabbed a little plastic bag. Opening it carefully, he held it up to the air, thinking it would fill up with fresh air which he could bring back to his polluted neighborhood.

Ramon Tecson was a garbage collector. He was doing his chore for the past twelve years, sorting out first class garbage from the rest and selling it to earn a living. One night, Ramon died in his sleep. When his body was found a few hours later, his nose, ears, fingers, were all gone; they were eaten by rats. Ramon slept on the ground with his community of garbage collectors — a hundred and twenty families — in an area equivalent to a vegetable patch in West Germany.

Many homes do not have floors. They use that same bare ground that was there when the Philippines was discovered by Magellan in 1521, living and sleeping at the mercy of rain, floods, snakes, bugs, concentrated urine. Adults use burnt rice for coffee, newspaper sheets for umbrella even during a typhoon, a congested canal for a public toilet, a pushcart for a home, usurers as solution to the lack of food and medicine, or as response to an unexpected occurence, like funeral. Most babies do not know what milk is unless they suck from the emaciated breasts of their mothers. Babies drink *ahm,* the water that boils while rice cooks.

Bodies grow stooped, accustomed to eating and working on the ground. Heads are used more to carry heavy baskets of bananas or soiled laundry than to learn. Children at an early age push carts to earn twenty-five centavos a day for the family's rice, scrounge for saleable garbage, spend nights vending cooked eggs and crunchy pork rind or *chicharon* along the bay where the drunk and the drug addict, the hold-upper and the rapist, also prowl.

In political life, slum dwellers have stories different from ours. There is the story of Renato. He was a member of an anti-US military bases coalition. One evening,

together with his friend, he started pasting anti-bases posters on a wall near Leveriza, our slum. That night, Renato did not go home. Two days later, he was found in an open field, hands and feet tied, body bludgeoned, spine seriously injured. His friend was dead. Renato alleges the military did this to him. Of course, the military denied it and that was the end of that tragedy.

Frank was a victim of a hold-up. Like a good citizen, he immediately reported the incident to the Makati police. He was finger-printed, interrogated, manhandled, and electrocuted by the police who were forcing him to confess that he himself stole the money. Frank refused to confess. He was detained for three more days in a cell with criminals, suffering more torture. He was released only when Catholic Sisters intervened. Frank left the prison with the warning that if he were to tell anyone about what happened to him, the police would find and kill him.

Yes, in this slum of Leveriza, Metro Manila, which once was a place by Manila Bay with pathways and fruit trees and public toilets clean enough for the Spanish *señoras* to avail of, we experience such human cruelty with no signs of waning. With rebels and revolutions, shifts in societal systems, changes in colonizers and Filipino presidents, even with the 1986 EDSA event, life for the urban poor remains most oppressive. What happened? What is happening?

It is quick to point out at one or the other — to our Spanish *conquistadores*, to our American educational system, to our Government's dismal confusion in the choice of priorities.

It is equally easy to point to over-population and to the Filipino's *mañana* habit as roots of the problem. Instead of accusing others, questions grip us. These, I share with you.

How could and why does the democratic system spew such masses of marginalized persons? How could a Christian populace, of which our country owns eighty-eight percent, arrive at such gross indifference to one's neighbour? Why, despite United Nations, summit meetings, the Pope, the Red Cross, the World Council of Churches, do international policies push the hungry to become more hungry, the filled to become over-full? Why is there only a whimper of protest and not global outrage against mass murder (militarization), race extinction (nuclear arms), international usury (debt crisis of Third World nations)? Why is national security dominant over people's security?

These world issues trickle down, shaking families which refuse to become still. The majority are legions, but the minority have the power. The rich can be wasteful, the poor are waste. Democracy can promote inequality among persons and nations. Christianity blesses those hands who give to the Church and tolerates what the rest of the body does to its neighbor.

Leveriza, ten years with a suffering faceless poor, struggles to survive, gasps to live what we call "faith."

The conflict is not between the capitalist and the communist, but between developed countries and the Third World; not between north and south continents, but between the north and the south of the same land; not between Christians and pagans, but between greedy Christians and Christians denied of their power.

Fishes swim in water; pump out the water and the fishes die. Wild animals and birds thrive in forests; cut down the trees and these animals and birds become extinct. Tribes live on and by their ancestral lands; confiscate these lands and tribespeople become revolutionaries.

The urban poor have very little of things; but this little is even denied of them. The urban poor live on a minimum of soil, oxygen, water. This minimum is daily becoming less, because people with power have grown mad. The urban poor are choking. We are choking. We are losing our basic human right to life. With heads unbowed, we cling to each other, beyond seas, forests, and land. Together, we fight back.

Let There Be Life, Not Death

MARY LOU B. MARIGZA

Total war on the grassroots civilian population threatens the lives not only of citizens living in Third World countries but also the life and resources of the whole world. This concept is promoted on a global scale by United States militarists. Sad to say, the Aquino Government, which was catapulted to position by the power of the people and not of guns, brazenly implemented the Low Intensity Conflict as a declaration of war against insurgents.

For the past several months, the people of Northern Luzon continue to notice the alarming pattern of snuffing out life, affecting not only individuals but whole communities. Whenever people voice their protest against this scary phenomenon, authorities dismiss it as part of counter-insurgency operations. Vigilante groups created with the blessings of the authorities, including influential church officials, were given the task of wiping out the insurgency in their areas. In a single stroke, the authorities decided to arbitrarily use the law by creating a monster that is both judge and executioner.

Human rights violations used to be committed only against so-called public order violators, subversives or communists who are favorite scapegoats in justifying militarization. But the recent killings of recognized leaders of people's organizations indicate a frightening trend. Tribal leader Ama Daniel Ngayaan of the Cordillera People's Alliance was killed in retaliation for the failed ambush of Conrado Balweg and his men in the CPLA. (The Cordillera People's Liberation Army or CPLA, led by Balweg, is the glorified vigilante group in the Cordillera that was legitimized by President Aquino at the Mount Data peace negotiations in 1986.)

Atty. David T. Bueno of the Ilocos Norte-Laoag City Human Rights Organization was murdered soon after the ambush of Lt. Col. Pablico and his men, and after a series of successful offensives by the New People's Army in Ilocos Norte. Vicente Labasbas of the *Bagong Alyansang Makabayan* was kidnaped and is still missing soon after a military patrol was totally wiped out in Aguilar, Pangasinan, an area supposedly freed of NPA elements.

Operation Red Buster III was conducted by a brigade-size military formation because logging concessions could no longer be exploited by the rich logging businessmen. This was after the people of Apayao declared "Operation Lapat" — a total ban on logging as defense for their ancestral lands and forests.

San Mariano, Isabela was periodically bombed after a series of ambushes by the NPA resulted in the destruction of armed personnel carriers and the killing of military men. Evacuation areas were set up in Mangatarem, Dasol, Bangui, Flora, Conner due to dislocation after military operations.

Intelligence and surveillance activities against people's organizations are intensifying. Military agents are suspected to be guarding and tapping the telephones of houses and offices of these groups. Intelligence work is beefed up by the formation of vigilante groups with names like "Alsa Pamilya," "Alsa Bayan," "Crusaders," "Solidarity Movement."

A method which is becoming widespread is the use of deep penetration agents. DPAs, as they are called, are assigned to penetrate people's organizations either as active members or as staff/personnel of these offices. Exposing these DPAs before they could bring harm to the organizations is a tedious and delicate process.

The elimination of "unwanted" elements practically changed not only the vocabulary of authorities but also the whole psyche of the people. Anyone who would criticize any aspect of government is a communist and should be eliminated. No distinction is made as if they see a Red ghost at every turn.

This thinking is so pervasive that it even extended to the elimination of criminal elements. Known gang leaders or criminals out of jail are picked up from their hide-outs, their mangled bodies soon recovered in sacks several provinces away. Many times they are burned beyond recognition. One thing is common in these killings — they bear torture marks with barbarities like stuffing in the mouth the sex organs of the victims. This is a practice reserved earlier for suspected subversives only.

People's organizations already made their appeal to the authorities. The declaration of total war against the people, following the dictates of American militarists, will only reduce our nation to tombs and mourning. The creation of the vigilante monsters would revive the dreaded death gangs we tried to disband by enshrining in our Constitution the dismantling of these armed bands and groups.

The total war will only increase the rate of deaths in our barrios. The people are deep in poverty. They ask for land, but they are given guns. They ask for livelihood, they get bombs instead. They reel from the effects of a huge foreign debt, and they are confronted with brigade-sized military operations.

The mourning attire of the Ilocanos is a white band tied around the forehead and black clothes worn the whole year round. Will the people of Northern Luzon continue wearing their black and white attire as if they are in a black and white screen? Will the children of the North forever tremble at the sight of armed men in uniform? Will they continue this macabre game of flee-and-hide when they hear helicopters buzzing?

When will the authorities stop treating them like enemies? Is their life still sacred?

January 1988

Indigenous Women Struggle for Human Rights in the Cordilleras

GERALDINE L. FIAGOY

The Cordillera highland region in northern Philippines is considered a resource base. The Cordillera people, however, like other indigenous peoples throughout the world, can be called "victims of development." Government imposes development projects in the region as a policy to extract its natural resources. However, these projects disregard the well-being of the region's indigenous inhabitants.

By making people believe that the region would be developed with the entry of big business, the state is able to wield a free hand in the exploitation of the region's wealth. Only a few are benefited by those businesses while the majority remains marginalized. They are displaced from their communities and their sources of livelihood in the natural environment are destroyed.

The people struggle to protect their collective rights to their land and resources against military attempts to protect big business and so-called development projects. In the process, they become victims of countless human rights violations such as forced evacuation, hamletting, detention, torture, and even extra-judicial execution.

While the entire community suffers, the women in many instances become doubly burdened. Take for example the entry of Cellophil Resources Corporation (CRC) in Abra province in the mid-seventies. When the people expressed their opposition to the logging operations of CRC, they were called subversives and thus hunted down. Countless men were forced to go underground, while many others were detained. The women were left to care for family and fields. At the same time, they would regularly visit their husbands or children in military camps to bring them food and ensure that they are not brought to unknown places.

In a related case in the town of Tineg where the logging concession operates, the military commander ordered the villages to build wooden bridges to ease transport of logs. The construction took the men away from the fields, thus decreasing farm labor hands and, subsequently, production. The women again had to take their place to ensure the survival of their families and community.

Meanwhile, in the rainforests of Apayao where the Isnegs live, the people were forced to evacuate when their forest habitation was divided for exploitation among big businessmen and Marcos cronies. The self-sufficient Isneg communities were displaced. The indiscriminate logging also brought environmental destruction such as flashfloods and erosion destroying the natural habitat that forest dwellers depended on for survival.

The people's resistance and the entry of the New People's Army brought in military battalions and more human rights violations. Apayao became a battleground between the rebels and Government soldiers. The airstrip of Taggat Industries, a logging company, was used to launch strafing and bombing operations on villages suspected to be NPA-influenced. In this conflict, civilians were affected. Villages were abandoned. People who were accused of being NPA sympathizers moved deeper into the forest. Others were forced to move to cramped evacuation centers where poor conditions resulted in the spread of various diseases which affected mostly women and children.

The Isneg women, from the time Taggat Industries and other big concessionaires entered Apayao in the early eighties, suffered countless violations. During military raids into the villages where the men were tortured and even killed, the women (married or single) were raped·by the soldiers. Documented cases reveal that some women were violated of their dignity even in front of their children. One victim was an 18-year old girl in Paco Valley. She was on her way to the village when elements of the 17th Infantry Battalion of the Philippine Army chanced upon her. She was raped and then killed by the soldiers. Her decomposed body was later found by a fact-finding team which hiked to the area a few months later.

In 1986, the 48th Infantry Battalion of the Philippine Army conducted a military raid in Conner, Kalinga-Apayao. Gallib Langa, a young mother, died from bullet wounds when soldiers fired indiscriminately at the houses. Gallib left three children, the youngest of whom was still two months old.

Another development project imposed on the Cordillera people is the Chico River Dam. In the mid-seventies, the Marcos Government attempted to start this World Bank-funded project in the Mountain Province and Kalinga-Apayao.

When the workers of the National Power Corporation set up their work camps in Tomiangan, the women joined the men in dismantling the camps of the workers. They

walked 28 kilometers to the main office in Tabuk to deposit the tents and equipments. This was a sign that they did not want the dam to be built and that the workers should leave the area.

The militant resistance of the Kalinga people forced the state to send the military. But the people demanded for the withdrawal of the military from the Chico Valley because of its long list of human rights violations against the people. The implementation of the project was discontinued.

The Chico Dam experience portrays a people's militant struggle against an imposed development project. The women, despite their double oppression, refused to be intimidated and continued to resist the project which they knew would destroy their villages and, invariably, their culture.

Similarly in the early seventies, the Bontoc women of Mainit in the Mountain Province showed they could participate in a political protest to defend their ancestral land. When the workers of Benguet Corporation, a big mining concern, tried to dig tunnels in the Mainit mountains, the women confronted them with their bare breasts. The act signified that they had no respect for the men intruding their village. The terrified workers ran away, although they were pressured by the company to return later. The militant women again turned them away. Benguet Corporation never returned up to this day. The Mainit villagers are now benefiting from their gold resources as they themselves are the ones extracting them from the ores.

The extreme form of resistance the people resort to in asserting their rights is to join the rebel New People's Army. In Apayao, where militarization intensified with the entry of logging concessionaires, membership of women in the rebel army increased. The problems brought about by the Chico Dam also resulted in the recruitment of Kalinga women into the group, with the first women squad formed in 1979.

While the NPA engages in political work to increase its ranks, the violence spawned by militarization is found to be instrumental in the growth of the rebel population. Women and children whose relatives are tortured or summarily executed by the military see no hope in civilian life and become rebels themselves. Lone survivors, usually women and children, of vicious military raids in villages look for the NPA as they have nowhere else to go. The continuing imposition of "development" on the people help in raising the political consciousness of more and more indigenous women, to the extent that they themselves even resort to armed struggle in confronting their oppression.

June 1988

Relief and Rehabilitation Work:
New Approach in Human Rights Advocacy

MEMEN L. LAUZON

The existence of "internal refugees" is a new phenomenon in present Philippine realities. Noted as early as the 1970s, this phenomenon is a result primarily of the intensifying armed conflict in the countryside where whole families are being displaced from their communities.

Massive evacuations involving several thousands of families already occurred in Mindanao as Muslim rebels and Government armed forces continued to clash over the Moro problem. This led to the displacement of around 200,000 to 300,000 Muslim Filipinos who are now taking refuge in Sabah, Malaysia.

There were also families in the Visayan islands of Samar and Negros who were displaced from their homes due to military operations meant to flush out communist insurgents. As militarization reached a national scale, displaced families are now found in almost all parts of the country, including Metro Manila.

The ouster of former President Marcos did not end the problem of displacement. It became even worse and continues unabated to date. However, the "refugeeization" of Filipinos, especially in the countryside, continues to receive minimal public attention both locally and internationally. Statistics may show the extent and magnitude of the problem. These figures cannot, however, reflect the miseries and hardships of its victims, including women and children who comprise about 70-75 percent of the displaced population.

The problem of displaced families is a human rights issue. Displacement comes in two forms: forced evacuation and hamletting. It affects a wide range of civil, economic and political rights, both individual and collective. It is a transgression of people's rights to abode, life, liberty and property; the right to adequate standard of living and health. Concomitantly, women and children's rights are also trampled upon as families and communities are forced to evacuate.

Human rights advocacy in the Philippines, therefore, must include the promotion and protection of these rights. An essential component of this advocacy is exposing the problem of displacement to the larger community so that they can be enjoined in solving it.

Documentation plays a vital role in solving the internal refugee problem. But attention must also be given to the concrete needs of displaced families. They are only able to take their meager belongings with them as they retreat to safer grounds to seek refuge. Some are fortunate to have school buildings or churches as evacuation centers. But for others, the nearest sanctuaries would be the forests and caves. In either case, there is extreme inadequacy of food and clothing, lack of proper shelter, and absence of means of livelihood.

Those responsible for forced evacuations and hamletting of communities find justification in the belief that in any war situation, innocent civilians are inevitably affected.

Local residents who live in areas known to be rebel strongholds or suspected insurgency hotspots receive such treatment on mere suspicion that they are supporters or sympathizers of rebel forces.

Human rights advocacy entails hard work. One must persevere in invoking adherence to the 1986 Philippine Constitution, and to international laws governing situations of war and conflict such as the provisions of Protocol II additional to the August 1949 Geneva Conventions, the Universal Declaration of Human Rights, the International Convenant on Civil and Political Rights, and the International Covenant on Economic, Social and Cultural Rights.

The dismal condition of the victims should also lead to other areas of human rights work. Regardless of their political persuasion, basic welfare services must be extended to the victims before, during and after displacement. Their condition could extend to an indefinite period of time. This uncertainty renders socio-economic programs especially necessary.

Pointing an accusing finger to the perpetrators is not enough ...

Socio-economic program is a new field in human rights work needing further exploration. It is both engaging and challenging.

We often read in newspapers and reports stories of families being displaced from their communities. But one gets an entirely different feeling when one actually witnesses families trooping down from the hinterlands with their children, small bundles of personal belongings and, on some occasions, domestic animals tagging behind.

It is equally deplorable to see them herded in makeshift evacuation centers. Here, children lay bare on cold cemented floors, with no food to eat and no proper hygiene and sanitation facilities. This condition makes them, especially the children, easy prey to communicable diseases. Epidemics often arise in evacuation centers, leading to deaths even among adults.

Some internal refugees are so used to the ever-changing peace and order situation in their localities that they evacuate on impulse upon threats of imposing hostilities. Later they go back when they think that the situation is somehow back to normal. That this is now part of their daily existence is equally terrifying.

When the families return to their communities, they realize they no longer have homes to go back to. They find their houses either burned down or bombed in the conduct of military operations, or destroyed simply because of long periods of abandonment. Going back to their original villages would mean starting all over again. A once peaceful and tranquil community would be transformed to an idle, lifeless, decremented village.

Spending time with these families would mean listening to a litany of problems, from severe poverty to worsening political hostilities. Political hostilities aggravate the economic hardships which the families already face. It is not easy to simply console them under this situation and assure them that things will get better, when one is aware that the solutions to the roots of these problems are unforseeable.

... attention must also be given to the concrete needs of displaced families

Words of compassion are not enough when you see mothers breast-feeding their babies with tears in their eyes; when you see the menfolk with their furrowed foreheads wondering how to support their families and thinking about the farms and crops which they unwillingly abandoned; when you see half-naked children lying sick or simply playing around ignorant of events happening around them. School children find themselves in a classroom yet ironically no classes are held.

All these are vivid pictures of a desolate populace trapped in a situation not of their own making and liking. They are victims of a war not theirs and yet they are the ones losing. No amount of money can compensate their broken lives. Pointing an accusing finger to the perpetrators is not enough. The task now at hand is to relieve these families of the agonies of their plight and uplift their deplorable condition; to help them resume a normal and decent life, in their original places of residence or in any other place of their preference.

As a short-term assistance, the extension of relief goods such as food, clothing, medicines and other necessities like kitchen utensils, soap, and others is most urgent. The basic needs of the displaced families should be provided for the duration of their stay in an evacuation center. Because present Government assistance to the families is so minimal that it could last them for only three days, non-governmental efforts become necessary.

The Ecumenical Commission for Displaced Families and Communities (ECDFC) is one of the non-governmental organizations which provide assistance of this nature. The ECDFC is the only NGO which specifically helps displaced families in terms of relief services and rehabilitation programs. The rehabilitation program of ECDFC is for long-term assistance. It envisions the attainment of self-sufficiency and self-reliance among displaced families through livelihood projects and providing other socio-economic opportunities towards the growth and development of people.

These objectives may sound abstract and idealistic, but they kindle hopes for a better tomorrow. This program is not a "dole out" type of assistance. The beneficiaries of the project are organized. The financial assistance is given to them as initial seed resource. All resources available locally, whether material or manpower, are tapped and maximized.

Education or conscientization is an integral component of the rehabilitation program. A people-based and people-oriented program is the best term to describe ECDFC's work with displaced families. Providing knowledge and skills is part of this component. Families are prepared to undertake feasible projects on their own. Community spirit is developed to strengthen the families' organization and sense of belonging; in this process, their level of consciousness is raised as well.

Through ECDFC's program, displaced families can be empowered to cope with their difficulties and be prepared as well when they go back to their abandoned communities to pursue other productive activities. Since there is no assurance that the implementation of the project will not be hampered, it is imperative to bear in mind the ultimate goal to eradicate totally the root causes of displacement. Otherwise, we will find ourselves caught in the "weeds paradox" where we pull out some weeds and others in greater number sprout in no time.

Relief and rehabilitation work is an essential part of human rights advocacy. It is through projection of human rights issues that specific needs of people are known, thus, mobilizing people to action in responding to these needs. The victims themselves must be at the center of organizing and education work, so that they become aware of their rights and responsibilities.

Children's Rights:
Turning Vision Into Reality

Nelia Sancho

All groups of varying persuasions in Philippine society declare adherence to the principles outlined in the United Nations Declaration of the Rights of the Child. Both government and non-government agencies and groups make pronouncements that every child's well-being should be protected, that every child should be given the opportunities and the environment to enable him or her to develop in all respects of humanity, whether these be material or substantial, whether in abstract terms like love and understanding or, in concrete terms like schools and social security.

Our country, though, cannot boast of pleasant statistics when it comes to the care of the well-being of children. Children comprise at least half of the population of the Philippines, the same population in which seven out of ten families live below the level fit for human beings as, indeed, even Government records attest to.

The poverty situation in the Philippines, because of an unbalanced development model ruled over by foreign and elite interests, perpetuates a state of deprivation for Filipino children. One out of every five children suffers from second to third degree malnutrition. Infants and toddlers commonly fall ill of preventable diseases like pneumonia, measles and diarrhea. These diseases bring about a high incidence of child deaths.

Education is highly priced as a personal achievement in the Philippines. For most children, their lack of access to education is a bitter reality. Only six out of ten Filipino children finish their elementary grade. Only two out of 100 pre-school children can avail of early childhood education even if the Government is aware that this is the most critical time in a child's development. This does not mean that education can bring forth all the potentials of those privileged to reach higher grades. Formal education can both strengthen and condition children's acceptance of westernized values and sexist orientation. It alienates them further from the values of nationalism, pride and love of country.

In an economy where parents are either unemployed or underemployed, it is not surprising that out-of-school youths now number at least 1.25 million. In a society where the income of both parents are insufficient to feed their children no matter how hard and long they toil, children are forced to leave school and instead go to work to augment their families' income, or even to barely survive for themselves.

In the rural areas, children become unpaid family workers, domestic workers, farm help, or workers in foreign plantations where they receive exploitative, starvation wages. In the urban areas, children roam the streets, run after vehicles and pedestrians in dangerously busy city streets to sell candies, garlands, cigarettes. Some of them wipe the windshields of moving vehicles or provide security to parked cars. One may even find them holed up in some

p doing odd jobs and getting paid a pittance for
more than eight hours of work.

The tourism programs which the Government is banking
on to earn precious green bucks only invite pedophiles and
pimps from all over the world to sample a most susceptible
"product" or "commodity" — the child prostitute. Our
children are victimized as sex slaves and prostitutes. In
their young minds, sex is already presented as a commodity
for sale, themselves as products in the sex market.

Our country is in a state of war against itself, as one
Filipino writer puts it. Dissatisfaction with past and
present Government policies breed two insurgencies — one
by the National Democratic Front/New People's Army, and
the other, by the Moro National
Liberation Front which believe that
Muslims are marginalized by
the Filipino mainstream. This
condition exacts untold suffering on children. Ongoing
documentation being done by
human rights organizations con-
firms that children are intensely affected by massive militarization in the country. Children, whose parents or relatives
are suspected of having linkages or symphathies with
underground revolutionary groups, witness tortures, killings
and harassments. Oftentimes, children are the victims of
these acts themselves. In rural areas, children experience
the stress of military operations such as strafings, bombings,
food blockades and massive forced evacuations leading to
the displacement of thousands of families.

Children are forced to leave school to go to work to augment their families' income

In the midst of such realities, advocacy groups for children's
rights are organized to promote education and concerted
action against economic, social and political threats to
future generations. For many such organizations, an

approach to the concerns and problems affecting children carries the thinking that meaningful changes in the lives of children cannot fully take place unless the Filipino people, including parents and the children themselves, are made aware of the full extent and inter-relationship of the issues affecting their future. A number of non-governmental organizations (NGO) are engaged in programs that aim to develop strong advocacy for the realization of the rights of children in the Philippines.

One such effort is being carried out by GABRIELA, an umbrella organization and campaign center for women's issues. GABRIELA established a commission dealing with the children's issues to serve as the machinery through which the progressive women's movement undertakes work for the rights and welfare of Filipino children in distress. The GABRIELA Commission on Children and Family was first organized as a Committee on Children in 1984, and was re-established in February 1988. It aims to enable the women's movement to pave the way for a popular struggle to establish a society and government that will promote children's rights and welfare.

Women, who suffer from inequality and oppression themselves and who shoulder the principal responsibility of caring for and protecting children, have no other choice today but to address the equally, if not more oppressive, situation of children. GABRIELA's goal is to enable women to be active agents for change, to struggle towards a vision of peace, justice and liberation for women and children, and all others.

GABRIELA advocates and promotes children's rights through various channels in the mass media, through conferences, and through cultural presentations. It also utilizes active venues like mass campaigns to underscore its advocacy. Indeed, the women's movement in the Philippines is an emerging force in the struggle for children's rights and welfare in the country. A review of the series of activities and projects initiated by GABRIELA bears this out. These actions are geared towards public awareness of the varied situations of the Filipino child in the family, school, workplace and community.

In 1987, together with organized urban poor women living in slum areas, GABRIELA set up four children's centers which provide daily pre-school and playgroup services for children in the poor communities. GABRIELA works closely with Parent's Alternative, Inc., an NGO specializing on providing appropriate teacher training to grassroots-based child care workers. This coordination helps in developing the quality and ensuring delivery of services, in promoting children's education and welfare (including the development of alternative educational curricula and teaching materials), and in providing on-going, on-site and on-the-job teacher training and consultancy.

A series of Children's Empowerment Workshops was organized by women for children in 1988. The workshops tried to evoke from the children their own visions of society and their perceptions of the problems confronting them. These workshops were conducted monthly among children of GABRIELA members, special children who were witnesses to violent militarization in the countryside and picketlines, and children of urban poor women who experience the harsh effects of poverty. In March 1988, the Children's Empowerment Workshops reached out to the child workers of Negros, a sugar-producing province, and to the street children of Manila.

In April 1988, a forum was organized by women on child labor. The forum dealt with the exploitative dimensions of child labor and brought together NGOs working on child labor. GABRIELA also launched a "children of war" campaign in October to educate the public on the effects of militarization on children and to generate support for the child victims.

GABRIELA also established its own Children's Theatre Group. Through the children's cultural performances, GABRIELA members and the general public became sensitive to the plight and perceptions of children. A leading community theatre group, the Philippine Educational Theatre Association, conducted a week-long children's theatre arts training to prepare the children for self-advocacy through theatre.

Beyond Manila, however, more and more children continue to lead unknown dimensions of poverty and oppression. GABRIELA hopes to make their situation known further by sponsoring fact-finding missions. In March 1988, a fact-finding mission probed on the child labor situation in the sugar industry, focusing on the Negros region.

The probe made use of participatory research which involve the child workers. The case studies were documented and will be published in an illustrated primer on child labor for popular dissemination.

Women today have no other choice but to address the equally, if not more oppressive, situation of children

In 1989, the GABRIELA Commission on Children is organizing a series of seminars and public forums on various issues affecting children. To prepare for this seminar, its regional and provincial chapters are undertaking documentation of the human rights situation of Filipino children in the various regions of the country. Some of the specific issues to be highlighted are: child labor, child prostitution, *Amerasian* children (offsprings of US servicemen and prostituted women in Olongapo and Angeles), street children, children of war, children victims of incest and rape. There will also be a women's consultation to signal the campaign to set-up a Women and Children Refugee Program to give succor to the victims of militarization and displacement.

To respond to the needs of child workers, there is a plan to set up a Child Worker's Center in a slum area in cooperation with a community youth organization in Pasay. The Center will extend drop-in services to child workers, provide livelihood support projects, health and medical assistance, legal aid, informal education, and sponsor theatre activities to be participated in by the children.

Come 1990, in consultation with other NGOs, GABRIELA plans to hold tribunal to hear various cases of children's rights violations. This activity is aimed to further highlight specific violations and crimes against children so that the consciousness of the media, the public, the NGOs, and the Government can be raised to a level where it can make effective and concerted actions with regards to the plight of Filipino children.

GABRIELA develops linkages with other children-oriented organizations and institutions on both national and international levels. Aside from the Parent's Alternative, Inc., GABRIELA also relates and cooperates with the Children's Rehabilitation Center, the Institute for the Protection of Children, SALINLAHI (an alliance for children's issues), and with grassroots-based women's organizations nationwide, particularly those among the rural women, urban poor women and women workers.

Internationally, GABRIELA has ties with Children As Peacemakers Foundation, Child Workers in Asia, Defense for Children International, and the newly established Working Group on Children of the Asian Commission on Women's Human Rights.

During the Children's Rights Workshop series held in September 24, 1988, the children were asked to write letters to Mrs. Corazon Aquino, to children, and to parents.

A twelve year-old girl, Erni Myen de Jesus, who participated in the workshop, wrote the following:

"President Cory, I have a simple request to make from you and others in your government. I want that you stop the military abuse and harassment on our parents. They are not the only ones affected — but it is we, their children, who also suffer. It is my wish that you join us in our efforts to realize our rights."

To her fellow children, Erni asked:

"Please be in solidarity with us. Even if you are rich do not think of yourselves alone. Help those of us who are suffering."

To the parents, she wrote:

"We hope that you will always guide and protect us. Please do not neglect us — continue to help us realize our rights and work for justice for us children."

Simple wishes, simple dreams. Filipino women will see through thick and thin this crusade in defense of the rights of their children.

Contributors

FOREWORDS

Mercy Amba Oduyoye is the moderator of Programme Unit III [Education and Renewal] and Deputy General Secretary of the World Council of Churches (WCC) based in Geneva, Switzerland. Ms. Oduyoye is from Ghana.

Mary John Mananzan, OSB is the national chairperson of the GABRIELA National Coalition, a broad organization of 101 women's groups. She is the Dean of College of the St. Scholastica's College in Manila, where she is also director of its Institute for Women's Studies. She is also a member of the Forum for Interdisciplinary Endeavors and Studies (FIDES), the Ecumenical Association of Third World Theologians, (EATWOT), and the Association of Women in Theology (AWIT).

ARTICLES

Victoria Narciso-Apuan is a church lay leader who has been active in promoting basic Christian communities since 1978. She is founding member of the Christians for the Realization of a Sovereign Society (CROSS). She is a theology and social work instructor, and administrator at Miriam College in Diliman, Quezon City.

Rosario Battung, RGS is a Good Shepherd Roman Catholic sister. She is a member of FIDES and EATWOT. Her contribution in this volume was written with **Wilhelmina** and **Rodolfo Molina**, both community organizers among workers.

Victoria Corpuz, Evangeline Ram and **Cynthia Dacanay** are connected with the Cordillera Women's Education and Resource Center (CWERC). Ms. Corpuz is also the international relations officer of the GABRIELA National Coalition.

Miriam Ruth M. Dugay is a member of the United Methodist Church (UMC) and a former leader of the United Methodist Youth Fellowship. She was detained during the first few months of the Aquino Government, and was released from prison on December 21, 1987.

Sharon Rose Joy Ruiz-Duremdes is founding member of AWIT in Western Visayas, a Commissioner of the Human Rights Commission of the Baptist World Alliance, and secretary of the Asian Baptist Women's Union. A Convention Baptist, she is also the regional coordinator of the Western Visayas Ecumenical Council. Ms. Duremdes was arrested and detained in February 1985.

Corazon Estojero, Emily Garcia, Lorena Lopez, Milagros Reloj and **Erlinda Yandoc** are all members of Families of Victims of Involuntary Disappearances (FIND). FIND is a humanitarian association dedicated to the protection and promotion of interests of victims of forced disappearances and their families. It was formed in September 1985.

Geraldine L. Fiagoy is the executive director of the Cordillera Resource Center for Indigenous Peoples' Rights (CRCIPR).

Nena Gajudo is the executive director of the Living Faith Formation, based in Manila. Nena is a poet.

Carol Gamiao works with the CRCIPR. The original version of her contribution to this volume first appeared in the February-March 1988 issue of *Cordillera Currents* (Vol. 1, Nos. 3 & 4), a monthly supplement published by the CRCIPR.

Helen R. Graham, MM is a Maryknoll Roman Catholic sister. She teaches Scriptures at the Sisters' Formation Institute in Quezon City, and at the St. Mary's Theologate in Ozamis City in Mindanao. Sr. Helen is also a FIDES member.

Joy Hofer is a worker of the Mennonite Central Committee (MCC). From 1982 to 1987 she worked in the MCC headquarters as writer on Latin America and Africa. She lived in Davao City with her family for one year until 1988, where she took responsibility in overseeing the programs of MCC in Mindanao. Her piece in this volume reflects the years she spent in Guatemala from 1979 to 1982.

Cecilia C. Lagman is the mother of missing Hermon Lagman. She is the chairperson of the National Council of FIND.

Memen L. Lauzon is a program coordinator of the Secretariat of the Ecumenical Commission for Displaced Families and Communities (ECDFC) at the time of writing of her article in this volume.

Adul de Leon is national vice-chairperson for internal affairs of GABRIELA. She is also director of the GABRIELA Commission on Violence Against Women; and chairperson of Alliance Against Institutionalized Dehumanization (AID), an agency working on social issues related to prostitution. Adul is a well-known stage and TV actress who champions women's rights.

Elisa Tita Lubi is an ex-political detainee. She was illegally arrested last July 28, 1988 and detained together with criminal offenders at the Manila City Jail. She is director of the GABRIELA Commission on Women's Human Rights. She is convenor of the GABRIELA Commission on Women's Human Rights, and pioneered the establishment of GABRIELA's Women's Crisis Center. She leads GABRIELA's campaign to release women political prisoners.

Mary Lou B. Marigza is a member of the United Church of Christ in the Philippines (UCCP). She is currently connected with the Northern Luzon Human Rights Organization based in Baguio City. She is an ex-political detainee.

Edna J. Orteza heads the Christian education program of UCCP. She was head of the Center for Mindanao Missions based in Cagayan de Oro City where she lived for many years.

Marissa Piramide, OSB is a Benedictine Roman Catholic sister based at the St. Scholastica's College in Manila. She is currently finishing a graduate program in social work at the University of the Philippines, Diliman.

Rose Cerdeña-Quebral was administrative pastor of the Citadel Church of UCCP. She is member of AWIT and AID. She was part of the International Women's Jury of the First International Tribunal on Women's Human Rights Violations in the Philippines, March 1988. She was education coordinator of the Church-Based Consumers Movement.

Nelia Sancho is founding member of GABRIELA, where she was secretary-general for three years (1986-1989). She is director of the GABRIELA Commission on Children and Family. Ms. Sancho was chairperson of the organizing committee of WISAP '89 (Women's International Solidarity Affair in the Philippines). She is also member of the Board of Directors of the Center for Women's Resources; and chairperson of the Board of Directors of Parents Alternative, Inc. Ms. Sancho was among the senatorial candidates of *Partido ng Bayan* in the last congressional elections.

Evelyn Balais-Serrano is the deputy chairperson of the Task Force Detainees of the Philippines (TFDP). She was formerly TFDP's national program coordinator for Direct Services. She is commissioner for Asia/Pacific in the Human Rights Commission of the International Federation of Social Workers.

Carolyn Israel-Sobritchea is Associate Professor of Philippine Studies at the Asian Center, University of the Philippines, Diliman, Quezon City. She is a member of Kalayaan. She also works with Sr. Mary John Mananzan at the Center for Women's Studies based in

Brenda Stoltzfus lived in the Philippines from 1984 to 1989 during which time she worked with prostituted women in Olongapo. In 1985, she helped establish BUKLOD, a center for hospitality women in Olongapo City. She is currently living in Berkeley, California where she is working on a book about stories of women in the bars near the American bases in South Korea, Okinawa and Olongapo. She is also connected with the Mennonite Central Committee.

Irenea Tayag is the mother of Carlos Tayag. She is also a member of FIND.

Christine Tan, RGS is a Good Shepherd Roman Catholic sister. She was a member of the 1986 Constitutional Commission of the Philippines. She works with the Alay Kapwa Christian Community based in Malate, Manila.

Adora Faye de Vera is a former political detainee from Southern Tagalog. She is a member GABRIELA.

REVIEWS

Nelinda Briones is an ordained minister of the UCCP. She is currently the Program Coordinator of the Women's Desk of the National Council of Churches in the Philippines (NCCP).

Robert McAfee Brown is Professor Emeritus of Theology and Ethics at the Pacific School of Religion in Berkeley, California. He is author of many books.

Esther Byu is the executive secretary of the Women's Concerns Desk of the Christian Conference of Asia (CCA), based in Quezon City, Philippines. Ms. Byu is a Baptist theologian from Burma.

Anna Dominique Coseteng represents the 3rd District of Quezon City in the Philippine Congress. She hosts "Womanwatch," a weekly television program for and about women.

Aurora Javate de Dios is the managing director of Conspectus Foundation Incorporated, based in Manila. Conspectus is a non-stock, non-profit technical assistance and consulting organization providing professional and intermediation services for international, non-government, church-based organizations, government institutions, and private firms.

Elizabeth Ferris works as executive secretary for the Refugee Service of the World Council of Churches. Ms. Ferris comes from the U.S.A.

Priscilla Padolina is the executive secretary for Rural Women's Concerns for the Sub-Unit on Women in Church and Society of the WCC. Ms. Padolina is a United Methodist layperson from the Philippines.

June Rodriguez is a noted lay leader of the UCCP. She is the executive director of the Rural Enlightenment for Accretion in Philippine Society. She is also the Philippine member to CCA's Program Committee on Women's Concerns.

Debora Spini comes from the Italian Methodist and Waldensian Churches. Debora is an Executive Committee member of the World Student Christian Federation (WSCF) where she serves as coordinator of its Women's Commission.

Elizabeth Tapia, Ph.D. is an ordained minister of the UMC. She is chaplain and faculty member of Harris Memorial College in Antipolo, Rizal.

EDITORS

Liberato C. Bautista is coordinator of the Program Unit on Human Rights of the NCCP, and vice-chairperson of the Philippine Alliance of Human Rights Advocates (PAHRA).

Elizabeth B. Rifareal was program assistant of the Program Unit on International Affairs of the NCCP, and was Executive Committee member of the World Student Christian Federation (Geneva).

Reviews

The experiences and life-stories of our sisters in this book depict our oppression, yet NO longer allowing the powerlessness to own us!

Nelinda Primavera-Briones
Program Unit on Women
National Council of Churches
in the Philippines

Moving stories of witnesses to the suffering and struggles of women who search for their identities and advocate for human rights indeed reveal the Asian realities. Their voices and their deep sigh in saying 'No' to the patriarchal culture and oppressive structure challenge us to join them in the struggle for freedom and fullness of life.

Esther Byu, *Burma*
Women's Concerns Desk
Christian Conference of Asia

Anyone wanting to get a capsule account of the status of women as well as the human rights conditions in our country today must get this book and start reading.

This book is made more credible, especially on the aspect of women's experiences, feelings, thoughts and aspirations by the fact that it is the women themselves speaking. First hand accounts of women who have been victimized and violated are interspersed with essays of women's lives in the streets, slums, the Cordilleras, and the Bible. The stories of human rights violations are particularly real to me because I personally know some of the victims. I, too, suffered upon reading about the brutalities and indignities inflicted on them. But to quote from the book, "When others are shedding blood, what right have I to shed tears?"

Hopefully, this shedding of sacrificial blood will cleanse our country of all the injustices under which our people are still reeling. Then, these precious lives would not have been given up in vain.

The chorus of women's voices as contained in this collection is like the chorus of Greek tragedy, lamenting our society's unjust treatment of women and the continuous assault on the people's basic rights as human beings.

Hopefully, sooner than later, we can work closely together and have a truly just, egalitarian and sovereign nation. Only then can women's voices be transformed into a chorus of joy.

Nikki M.L. Coseteng
Representative
3rd District of Quezon City
Philippine Congress

In these stories one can see and feel the violations through the eyes of the victims and the powerless, and yet their message is so powerful. There is an urgent need to challenge the existing human rights concepts from the women's perspective and search for a new understanding of human rights. A book that is a "must" reading for every woman and man ... to become aware of the issues ... and to challenge the structures (and the churches) to take responsible action.

Priscilla Padolina, *Philippines*
Rural Women's Concerns
World Council of Churches

And She Said No! presents a Philippine view of what it means to be woman, to be fully human. It is a narrative theology that provides the readers with an understanding of the constant interplay between personal and social liberation in a Third World context.

This book affirms women from various sectors of Philippine society, known and not so well known, tribal and poor, urban and professional. The stories and analyses shared are creative and confrontational, gentle and powerful. Here are women resisting, saying No to powers-that-be; women writing their experiences of struggles and strength; women struggling for justice and peace, reclaiming identities; women working with people so their dreams will be fulfilled.

This is a valuable and timely contribution to emerging Asian women's theology. A must reading for both women and men, with a section for children as well. Warning: this book can change your life!

Elizabeth S. Tapia, Ph.D.
Development Center for Women
Harris Memorial College
Antipolo, Rizal

These are personal stories of pain and anguish, of unbelievable suffering and struggle. They are testimony to the courage and faith of so many Filipino women who somehow find the strength to go on, to resist, to keep hope alive. Reading the stories, and the analysis which places them in context, made me see the global connections of women's human rights work. In Central America and Southern Africa, in the Middle East and Indochina, women suffer imprisonment and torture, rape and forced prostitution, the agony of searching for disappeared relatives. This book adds an essential human dimension to our understanding of what it means to struggle for human rights in the Philippines — and in the world — today.

Elizabeth G. Ferris, USA
Refugee Service
World Council of Churches

The situation of Filipino women can be taken as the paradigm of the contradictions in Philippine society. Their lives speak of the struggling of their nation as a whole. This book is a witness to their growing awareness of the deep link between their liberation as women and the general struggle of their people for true justice.

This book reminds us that the structures of oppression affecting Filipino women are active all over the world; that "women" are not simply a part of something else, but a subject on their own; that their struggle is never just for themselves, but embraces general values.

The voices and the stories remind us in the First World about our responsibility, not in the trivial sense of guilt, but in the commitment to identify strategies of solidarity which start from struggle for justice in our own societies. Moreover, we are reminded that we in the countries of the north of the world are perpetuating the system whose effects are embodied by the concrete lives of women in this book.

"And She Said No." Indeed, there are many Nos to be proclaimed. Each of us has our specific No to say. This book is a precious help to identify ours.

Debora Spini, *Italy*
Women's Commission
World Student Christian
Federation

People's stories are an essential element in the development of a struggle. We should not be impatient or half-hearted in listening to the stories of a people, especially from those who toil to feed us.

In *And She Said No!* women are telling their stories. The stories they tell are real and disturbing. I hope that when you finally let go of this book, you will get up from wherever you are, look in the mirror, and tell yourself, "now I will be beside HER, and struggle for OUR rights".

June Rodriguez
Rural Enlightenment and
Accretion in Philippine Society

*The stories shared by every woman in this book —
activist, mother, worker, peasant, wife — eloquently reflect
the collective lament of a nation suffering from the ravages of
war and violence and its consequent human rights violations.
They help broaden our understanding of human rights that,
like so many other concepts, have made the plight of women
invisible.* **And She Said No!** *is more than just a negation of
the injustice of women's oppression. It is an affirmation of the
determination of Filipino women to redefine and reshape
their future.*

Aurora Javate de Dios
Conspectus Foundation, Inc.
Philippines

*The "up" side of these stories is that despite the past
oppression women have suffered in the hands of men and,
therefore, the legitimacy of extrapolating from past oppression
to present oppression (a history that would justify eternal
enmity between the sexes), many of the stories in this book
breathe out the extraordinary love that some women feel for
some men, and how extraordinarily courageous are some of
the risks they are willing to make for those they love. That's
humbling beyond any telling of it. But amid much that is evil
and sordid, it is our source of hope for the future.*

Robert McAfee Brown, *USA*
Pacific School of Religion
Berkeley, California